IGNITE
your
TEAM

JC BERNSTEIN

IGNITE *your* TEAM

USING THE *Spark Method* TO LEAD, INSPIRE, AND BUILD A TEAM THAT CARES

Contact information for Crescent Heights Publishing–crescentheightspublishing.com

ISBN: 979-8-9875212-0-5 (paperback)
ISBN: 979-8-9875212-1-2 (ebook)
ISBN: 979-8-9875212-2-9 (hardcover)
ISBN: 979-8-9875212-3-6 (audiobook)

Printed in the United States of America

Ordering Information:
Special discounts are available on quantity purchases by corporations, associations, and others. For details, contact jcbernstein.net

This book is dedicated to my first born son, Collin.
Because of you I know the meaning of motivation and purpose.
Love you, bud.

Table of Contents

How I Lost and Found My Spark

"IT'S SO HARD to find good help these days."

I hear that complaint from so many of my fellow managers, and every time I hear it, I smile, shake my head a little, and think, "Maybe the problem isn't the help at all."

Look around. Today, social influencers make millions by sharing their favorite lip gloss on Instagram, and side-hustles can make billionaires out of high school dropouts. So why should anybody want to find a traditional job anymore? And why should anybody stay in a job when they can find another one that pays a little more right down the street? Those are good questions. Perhaps the answers lie in why hiring has turned into a bidding war in which leaders today are being asked to find new methods to attract and keep their most valuable resource—their people.

Even moderately successful managers know that the numbers on their P&L are a direct reflection of their people's performance. Your employees are the arms, legs, and minds behind innovating new processes that make your company more proficient and innovative. Your people can be your failure, or they can be your success. You must treat them with as much care and respect as you would a customer.

No doubt you've heard that assertion before, but it's not just a cliché. In my 10 years as a boots-on-the-ground General Manager for a national chain of family restaurants, I was taught to share the "why" of every task. Beyond that tactic, I thought that bringing people into my company's mission statement would make people feel purposeful and personally invested in their work. The theory goes that when people understand why they are doing something, they will be motivated to do a better job. But it's just a theory. The reality? It doesn't work like that.

Here is the truth: People only undertake an action enthusiastically to fulfill what matters to them, not what matters to you. Even if they adore you, even if your staff feels driven to live up to your expectations, they will work to achieve your objectives primarily because of how your approval and praise make them feel. They feel good about themselves when they have made you proud, and their underlying drive is always how their performance affects them. Understanding how deeply rooted that concept is ingrained in us is the most valuable knowledge a leader can possess.

Since people are motivated by the things that are most important to them, we as leaders have to tap into that knowledge, see it, acknowledge it, and feed it whenever and however we can. Expecting people to be motivated by anything that does not directly impact what they hold valuable is like pressing on the gas pedal without first turning on the car: you won't get anywhere.

I am not suggesting that you cater to your employees' every need. That advice would be ludicrous. You are still the boss, and you have standards that you have to uphold. Instead, I am saying that in order to influence their will to work, you must connect the work you need them to do with what matters the most to them.

How is that possible, you ask?

Handcuffs Shackle Performance.

Let me share a story with you.

From the second that I stepped into management, I had a burning drive to succeed. I didn't need much coaching. I was every manager's dream employee. I took the initiative. I was proactive and completely self-motivated.

For nine years, I was the poster child for productivity and professionalism. I followed all protocols to the letter. I didn't let anything get in the way of doing precisely what the company needed me to do, and I checked all the boxes on my way to the next leadership level. I understood the critical importance of finding out what mattered to each and every one of my employees, and I did what I needed to do to keep their fire blazing. And then, nine years into my meteoric rise to the top, my spark went out. *Poof*. All my motivation and momentum came to a screeching halt. Just like that, it was all gone.

I could not understand what had happened to me. I was still the same model employee I had always been. I was still proactive and professional. I still needed my job. Nothing about me had changed. I was in the top GM spot in my company. I was responsible for training all new managers and was making more money than I ever had before. I should have been on fire, more motivated than ever. But I had never felt more uninspired. The spark in me was dying out, and people started to take notice.

When I finally figured out what changed, I realized it wasn't me—it was my manager. You see, I had taken over a new location and begun to assess what improvements could be made. And there were plenty. But this new location was also my boss's pride and joy, and there were a select few employees he had a soft spot for. When I attempted to make some adjustments to my store to improve it, my boss shut me down. Instead of trusting my judgment, he was shaken up by a select few who resisted the change—his favorites—and told me not to "rock the boat." I felt handcuffed by his unwillingness to listen to my suggestions and have my back.

His control left me feeling useless and uninspired. I was no longer able to build the kind of high-performance team I had become known for building in the past because I wasn't given the freedom I had had before. I felt reduced to being an operator rather than a leader. My manager was like a fire extinguisher, snuffing out the inner fire that had fueled my motivation and my success.

The experience taught me more about being a manager and a leader than all of my successes combined. I learned how easy it is to turn a model employee into a problem player by failing to understand what makes a person tick.

It was during that difficult time in my work life that I developed the SPARK Method. This system allowed me to take the ideas that had worked for me and apply them to my teams. And SPARK can work for you, too.

The SPARK Method

FOR MANAGERS TO build motivated, high-performing teams, they need motivated and high-performing players. Not just one or two, but every member, to some degree, has to be motivated and put in effort. Without motivation and effort, you get employees who are undependable and disconnected and who spend more time chitchatting or zoning out on their favorite social platforms than working on assignments or being attentive to your customers.

All it takes is one lower-performing, unmotivated employee to pull down the rest of the team. Even the most motivated of employees will lower their standards if they are surrounded by others who don't put in equivalent effort. The more time a high performer spends working alongside an underperformer, the less motivated the high performer becomes. They begin to think things like:

+ That guy wasn't on time, so why should I be tomorrow?
+ They didn't complete their work the way we were taught to, and the boss didn't seem to care. So why should I put in the extra effort to do it right?
+ No one else cares about setting up for a successful shift, so the whole shift suffers, and we are all miserable. Why should I be the only one to put in the work? Maybe I will just look for another job.

It is easy to focus only on the motivated. The already-motivated listen. They take feedback and run with it. They try. We feel like we are getting somewhere when we work with the easily motivated. But when we only focus on the already-motivated, the road to building a high-performing team composed of equally high-performing players becomes longer. The longer we focus only on the motivated and put off motivating the undermotivated, the longer those managers will spin their wheels trying to build out an exceptional team. Simply put, we are missing a huge portion of the population.

I understand why managers shy away from trying to motivate those who don't seem to care. Motivating people feels hard. It can feel like a daunting task to have to invest so much time in people who don't seem to care when so much is already on your plate. But it doesn't have to be.

We assume that motivating the unmotivated is impossible because everything we have been taught about motivating hasn't worked. We've been told to share the purpose behind our work, the mission, and our collective goals to make the team feel like their effort has a purpose, a cause. We hope that making someone feel like they are contributing to something meaningful and bigger than themselves will magically inspire them to want to work. But the truth is that those approaches aren't enough. They are not enough because those "motivating" concepts have everything to do with the company and nothing to do with our employees.

The harsh reality is that most people don't deeply care, to their core, about your work or your goals. But all people do care about their individual goals, their purpose, their values, and their mission.

We know that in many industries, especially those that are

customer-facing, your company's objectives typically have nothing to do with your employees' goals, passions, and purpose. So, as a manager, if you want people to care about your work, you have to balance out the scale. Spend less time focusing on trying to make them care about your mission and replace much of that time with learning about them and their goals. The secret is to understand what they value, what they strive to accomplish, and what they find meaningful, and to connect your objective to theirs. And believe it or not, those things aren't that difficult to figure out.

Understanding your employees doesn't require long, expensive, and specialized team-building meetings or dramatic heartfelt conversations. It is as simple as this: *talk to them*. Periodically, throughout the day, as you prepare for meetings, as you work alongside them, as you pass them on your way to lunch, take a few moments to get to know them, little by little, so that you can weave what they care about into their day-to-day work.

But what do you say? How do you make that personal connection a habit? How do you do it well without it being awkward? And how in the world do you connect what you need them to do at work to an individualized value or priority? The concept might sound overwhelming at first, but that's just because it is different, and you haven't yet learned it.

Don't be scared away by a foreign concept. The truth is it is very simple. So simple, in fact, that I have broken it down into five easy steps that any manager can follow in order to connect with their employees easily and effectively. In the rest of this book, I will give the details of what each step involves.

Here are the steps to the appropriately named SPARK Method:

S: Slow Down to Gain Perspective
P: Pay Attention
A: Ask Calibrated Questions
R: Read the Response Signs
K: Know How to Connect

If you follow this method step by step, you will create a better and more productive relationship with your staff and will understand what excites and motivates every individual on your crew. Not only that, but the quality of your communications will improve and inspire so that you can build and maintain a productive, engaged, high-performance team, whether you are running a small local restaurant or a global company that employs thousands.

The SPARK Method will help managers at every level to achieve success by teaching you how to identify what is most important to your employees, connect that drive and aspiration to the work they do, and give your employees a reason to provide top-level performance consistently over time. The bonus for your employees—and ultimately for you—is that they are rewarded with something that is more valuable than money: a sense of connection and happiness on the job.

I have already taught many to find success with this method. You are next.

Are you ready? Let's get started.

Step 1:

Slow Down To Gain Perspective

ONE OF MY children was born four months after my promotion into a GM role. I was a high-risk pregnancy, so I was placed on bed rest about three months before my due date. When I left, the store was rockin'. Sales were up, customer service was fantastic, and I flashed numbers that caught the executive team's attention constantly. My team was phenomenal.

Between bed rest and maternity leave, I was out for four or five months. And I will never forget the day I came back. I could barely recognize the place. The restaurant was a mess, and the tenured, awesome team I had built was almost all gone. Most of the team I had hired, trained, and motivated had quit because of bad management and a now-poor work environment. In fact, half of the roster included names I had never seen before. Standards had fallen, and the numbers reflected just how far down the fall had been.

While I was out, our district had realigned, and now I had a new boss. I had never met him before, and I worried about what he would think of me. I couldn't let him believe that these were my standards. The current state of the restaurant was not a reflection of me or my leadership. My core group was still there (thank goodness!), and they helped me hunker down and execute a plan to get the place back on track.

The to-do list was long, and it would take time and manpower to get things back to where they needed to be. But I was fortunate to have a group of people who cared deeply about the restaurant's success, and they were committed to helping me turn the place back around.

We were on a mission. It was "go time"! We kept our eye on the prize.

For weeks, my team worked tirelessly: scrubbing, organizing, retraining, painting. You name it, and they stepped up and did it. As soon as one item on the checklist got completed, it was on to the next. There was no time to waste to get the place back in shape. I had to show this new boss what this team was made of and the standards we stood for. One project at a time, we built our restaurant back. It didn't happen overnight, but we eventually got back to operating like a well-oiled machine.

But it almost didn't happen.

One day, about two-thirds of the way through the project, one of my most reliable employees, Emma, came to see me. "JC, can we talk?" she asked.

"Of course," I replied.

From the look on Emma's face, it was clear that something was bothering her. "JC, listen, we love you, but all you ever do is talk to us about our numbers and give us cleaning assignments. When was the last time you asked V about her classes or Steve about his kids? It feels like you are just working us to the bone, and we are just numbers to you now."

Emma's feedback was tough to hear because she was 100%

right. For weeks, I had been focused only on the to-do lists. I had assigned my team tasks, critiqued their work, and layered on more and more. I had been treating my team like workers and not like people I knew and liked and cared about. I hadn't taken the time to just talk to them, to understand what was going on in their lives, to check in on what was most important to them.

The team was still working hard, but the dynamic was different. They weren't upbeat, they weren't interacting on shift. The vibe had changed. It was quiet, and they weren't working with passion anymore. They were even interacting with the customers differently; they were being less attentive, less friendly, and their smiles were forced. It seemed like everything about work, even the customers, was a chore that they had to deal with.

The restaurant was getting cleaner, yes, but the dynamic of the team was suffering. And I knew that if I didn't have their dedication and their passion, my results would be short-lived, and the team would eventually dissolve.

The realization hit home, hard. I had been focusing on fixing everything that was wrong to show my new boss how great we were, and I had forgotten to see the people who were getting the job done. My team had noticed the difference and felt neglected.

If this team was going to work at their former caliber, they needed me to see them again, and they needed to see me. Before I had left on maternity leave, my crew had been excited to come to work. They had loved working together. The team environment had been cohesive, connected, and positive. They had worked hard and knew exactly how that hard work contributed to the success of the business. And it benefited them, too. They loved coming to work, and they took pride in doing their jobs well. But now, we were disjointed. My employees needed me to remember that they weren't robots—and that I wasn't a robot, either.

The experience taught me a valuable lesson: it's easy to get bogged down with executing tasks. As with anything, when we only focus on one thing, we lose sight of others. When that thing we lose sight of is our people, then the driving force behind what makes every business succeed starts to fall out from under us.

To ensure that decline doesn't happen, you have to slow down, even stop for a minute. Give yourself a chance to zoom out, notice, and understand the totality of what is happening around you.

CHAPTER 1

Put the Need for Speed on Pause

WE LIVE IN an era where speed is considered a necessity. Immediate access to information is the expectation, frictionless service is a requirement, and convenience to all things is essential in order to keep up. Removing barriers that inhibit speed feels essential because there is a constant need to get more done in less time. In our minds, the more we do, the closer we get to accomplishment. The more things we accomplish, the more productive we are, and the more productive we are, the more successful we become.

To become more productive, everyone is packing their calendars, double-booking meetings so they can maintain momentum and get there faster. We multitask and look for shortcuts. We listen to books on Audible while driving instead of carving out time to read. To shorten the learning curve more, we even have summaries of text available through apps, maximizing the amount of information we can absorb in a fraction of the time it would otherwise take. We have a never-ending amount of information available at our fingertips, and more and more barriers to learning and doing are removed for us daily.

Customers reinforce this need for speed. Their calendars are just as packed as ours. And companies have met their customers' speedy demands. Just ask Target or Walmart, which quickly saw the need to change their delivery options in order to keep up with Amazon Prime's free two-day shipping. Buy Online, Pick Up In Store (BOPUS) was invented to support busy consumers with a streamlined service, thereby limiting the amount of time they had to spend in stores and sparing them the inconvenience of waiting in line. The pandemic streamlined this speed of service even more by pushing stores to offer curbside delivery. Now we don't even have to get out of our cars!

The customer now equates speed with value, and the fastest wins. The computer with the fastest processer becomes the new hot buy. The fastest internet service gets the subscriber. The quickest delivery time wins the purchase. We expect things to be available to us at our fingertips, and businesses must meet the demand in order to survive. COVID made the playing field clear: Businesses that remained agile and adapted quickly survived; those that didn't failed.

How do those conditions translate into a manager's day-to-day? Companies depend on their managers to drive productivity and speed in each location. Their support is incredibly important because, as we have seen, speed is essential for keeping a company relevant in business. The manager is the driver of efficiency and meeting customer expectations. Therefore, the responsibility of execution lies on the manager's shoulders. You have to keep moving to meet the demand. Results that aren't delivered fast enough are associated with failure: not being good enough, not hitting the standard. And the stakes are high, which puts a lot of pressure on managers. The potential for failure is very stressful to navigate.

The Physical and Emotional Impact of Speed.

When you are running hot, firing on all cylinders all the time, you are more reactive than you would normally be. All your senses are heightened at this pace, and your nerves are very close to the surface. It's anxiety-producing to run this fast over long periods of time, to be fearful that you won't make it to the finish line, that you will fail.

This can bring on feelings such as disappointment, shame, frustration, or anger.

Many managers lean into this fear, using it as fuel to drive their endurance in the speed race. The theory is this: if you plow through, unaffected by resistance, you will have succeeded, thereby avoiding failure and shame. But this comes at a cost. Working at that pace and operating under those circumstances creates a real risk of burnout.

Kelly's Story

Kelly is a manager who understands burnout better than anyone. She had been the General Manager of a big-box retail store for many years, holding that position throughout the COVID-19 pandemic. Kelly is just one example of how extremely difficult the virus's disruption to business was for many managers in many industries.

Like many others, Kelly had a very difficult time trying to staff her store. Employees didn't feel safe working during the pandemic, so they quit. Some chose not to work so that they wouldn't be exposed to the virus, and never-before-seen unemployment benefits made it possible for those workers to stay home. Others left because of a nonstop bidding war with other companies over wages.

The chaos was hard on most managers, and Kelly was no exception. She would hire someone at what she thought was a very high wage, and the next day they would leave for more pay and a sign-on bonus from a competitor. It was an impossible dynamic to keep up with. Despite Kelly's best efforts, she was just spinning her wheels. She was lucky if 10% of the candidates she scheduled for interviews even showed up.

While Kelly was struggling to staff her store, she faced the very real problem of being shorted merchandise off the truck, so space she had planned to fill was suddenly empty. If she and her team didn't quickly reimagine their plans to set up a department, the store might look like it was going out of business.

And then there were the customers. They were angry and demanding. The company mandated a mask policy, and it wanted the staff to enforce the policy with customers. Many customers reacted badly. They would scream at employees and get in their faces, and some even pushed fixtures over.

It was an exhausting climate in which to work. Worse, because the staff was so lean, Kelly had to work close to 80 hours a week just to keep the doors open. Kelly finished her shifts exhausted, and things weren't any less stressful when she got home. She had a husband and two young kids. Her husband had been laid off, and the kids were on remote learning. They were younger, five and seven, so sitting down and reading from a computer screen for five hours wasn't a realistic option for them. Her husband was overwhelmed, rightfully so, but Kelly was too cranky and worn out to help him out. Her work had demanded so much of her that she was neglecting her family. It was a perfect storm.

One day, after working an 11-hour day, Kelly came home and her husband gave her an ultimatum: "Either you quit your job, or I leave." The threat scared her, and for hours, Kelly and her husband discussed the problem. They agreed that Kelly needed to at least take some time off of work. She decided that she had no choice but to ask her boss for a leave of absence for one month. It was either that, or she would have to resign.

Kelly was hopeful that her boss would support her request for some time to regroup and refocus. Thankfully, he did. She took the time she needed to slow down and regain her bearings, both with her family and for herself, and she returned to work ready to pick up where she had left off. This time, when she walked into her store, she had a game plan for each day, a newfound perspective on the magnitude of her job, and a realistic acceptance of what she could take on and what she couldn't.

As Kelly learned, burnout at work will spill over into your personal life. The need for speed and fear of failure will guilt you into feeling like you have to be 100% available and on call all the time. So, you take every call as it comes in. There is a pressure to read and respond to emails immediately so as not to miss anything and to show leadership that you are in control. Such focus makes it impossible for you to disconnect, unwind, and recharge. Through dinners, birthday parties, and social events—special moments you will never get back—you stay tuned in and in constant working mode.

Over time, the pace will inevitably start to affect your mood, patience, and friendliness with family and friends. Your short fuse will rear its ugly head in unwarranted moments, and relationships may start to suffer. You may even start to view your partner, family, or friends as just another barrier to overcome or another area in your life to manage, and you will start to treat them that way.

The constant go-mode mentality will start to take its toll, and, like I did, you will also lose your spark at work. Suddenly, getting up to start your day will be a real drag, and it will be a job in itself just to pull yourself out of bed. You will start to put in the bare minimum just to get through the day and justify not getting fired. Your results won't motivate you anymore. You won't be able to care less about being at the top of the pack. Being somewhere in the middle will do just fine.

 Most of our employees have terrible timing. It seems like when they want to talk to you about something, they inconveniently approach you when you literally have 15 things going on. Don't shoo them away. Find a better time to talk so you can listen to them later.

The Physics of Faster, Faster, Faster!

If you're only ever in go mode, your staff will perceive that you're too busy, and, therefore, that you're unapproachable. You may begin to seem unavailable or even intimidating to the very people you are trying to connect with and motivate. Your inattentiveness to your staff may start a chain reaction. Here's how that scenario unfolds:

1. Your team stops asking questions, so they take longer to figure things out or they make mistakes.
2. Productivity declines.
3. Your team starts missing deadlines because the environment doesn't feel supportive or positive and people aren't excited about being there.
4. People begin to show up late, or they begin calling out. On the surface, it starts to appear as though they just don't care anymore. The details that they miss start to affect the customer.
5. Complaints start to roll in, sales start to decline, and other key performance indicators (KPIs) fall out of line.

6. You start to burn out and become discouraged.
7. The death spiral picks up speed, and suddenly you're moving fast in the wrong direction.
8. You hit the ground running, and not in a good way.

Fortunately, there are some warning signs before you go into a death spiral that you cannot reverse. Just like pilots flying at high altitudes without visual cues and with little margin for error, it all starts with a checklist that you can touch base with from time to time, which will tell you when you need to adjust your flying speed. We will review those steps in just a moment. But first, understand this...

Stress Kills Good Leadership and Good Leaders.

Constantly operating in a heightened state is stressful. Just like a car left running for hours, we can overheat and break down on the side of the highway. Pistons may crack, wires melt, parts warp. Soon, the whole engine dies. The same is true for you. Unfortunately, many managers overlook how being in constant motion makes it harder to meet their goals and can put a dent in their leadership skills.

When you are constantly rushing, your judgment is bound to suffer. We miss a lot and cut corners just to get the job done. We begin to overestimate what we know and underestimate what we don't. Such problems are a natural side effect of speed because we feel like we need to figure things out quickly, solve problems rapidly, and get ourselves back on task. Quick assumptions can lead to errors in judgment that can be disastrous.

Say, for example, that you assume someone is mad at you because they didn't smile at you when you walked in the door. This might sound like a trivial matter, but thinking that an employee is mad at you and not knowing why can lead to misunderstandings and even to resentment on the job. In your hurry to associate their mood with you, you didn't even consider that they might have another reason they weren't in the mood to smile at anybody at the moment. Your rushed state and hasty judgment directly affected your interpretation of their action.

Making sound decisions and reaching reasonable conclusions with *all* of the information is essential. Decisiveness is an essential competency in management. After all, that's why they pay you the big bucks! The state of the business, the loyalty of the customers, or the well-being of your staff might depend on the conclusions you draw and the decisions you make from those conclusions. If you are moving too fast to collect all of the relevant information, you aren't positioned to make sound decisions.

Emotions can also run high when you are in a prolonged state of motion. When you are tired, you can get testy, and that effect can cloud your lens. You might tend to perceive things as personal when, in fact, they aren't. Anger or frustration might lead you to become reactionary instead of thoughtful in your responses and decisions.

Speed also diminishes your analytical judgment. Analysis requires time to process the facts, to think through potential scenarios, and to consider possible outcomes. When you don't allow yourself the time to consider the whole picture, you bypass crucial steps and just make a call. You also can't be sure that it's the call that will bring you closer to your goals. In fact, sometimes an uninformed decision can veer you further off track.

Once a team has completed a project, give them time to recover. When we give too many tasks back-to-back without breathing time in between, employees will get burned out and stop wanting to try.

Worse, operating for too long in a heightened state of urgency can negatively impact your health. Working that way requires you to stay in a constant state of stress, which has a very real, clinically proven effect on your body. Some side effects seem recoverable at first, like an inability to fall or stay asleep, resulting in temporary fatigue, but these are just the first warning signs. Long-term stress without rest and recovery results in serious health conditions, some of which may not be reversible.

Working Faster Isn't the Same as Working Smarter.

When in a position of leadership where the results fall on your shoulders, the idea of slowing down even for a second feels counterproductive and scary. But, as Kelly's story teaches us, operating in a constant state of motion comes at a cost. Being busy isn't the same as being productive. When we dedicate all our time and energy to racing around to get everything done faster, we lose our bigger vision and our effectiveness as leaders.

Learning when and how to slow down is the first step in becoming more effective leaders.

Checklist for Managers Ready to Hit the Wall:

+ Do you arrive to work energized and ready to take on the day? Or does the thought of walking through those doors feel draining?
+ Is your team productive and engaged? Or do they procrastinate?
+ Do your employees show up consistently? Or do they call out or even quit?
+ How is customer service doing? Are your customers happy, leaving great reviews, and coming back for more? Or are you finding yourself fielding complaints, resolving mistakes, or apologizing for poor service?
+ On the employee side, do you find yourself having to dedicate more and more time to resolving complaints?
+ What is the status of your KPIs like sales, labor, customer satisfaction ratings, or other key metrics your business focuses on? Are they showing growth or are they declining and becoming harder to manage?
+ Are you able to disengage when you leave work and spend time on the things in your personal life that matter to you?

Or do you find yourself having to cancel appointments with yourself or your friends and family to attend to work matters?

The moral of the story when it comes to speed is that sometimes you absolutely must slow down. Slowing down in the right moments will allow you the time to take an honest inventory of the current state of your business, the processes that drive it, and the adjustments you might need to make to be successful.

Time gives you the opportunity to assess what you might be missing or overlooking. It gives you an opportunity to truly hear and understand what is going on around you. It creates space for you to completely and granularly audit the quality of work that your team is producing. It allows you to identify patterns and warning signs that might slow your business down unexpectedly. It gives you the situational awareness that all leaders need to accomplish their mission.

Key Takeaways:

- Speed is the expectation, and we feel pressure to deliver faster.
- Running too hot for too long creates stress and burnout and makes you sick.
- Operating at a high speed makes you seem unapproachable and unavailable to your team.
- Working faster isn't the same as working smarter.
- If your team stops showing up ready to work, if you start feeling the effects of burnout, it is time to slow down.

CHAPTER 2

You Have to Slow Down to Move Fast

IT IS ONLY natural for a manager to feel like there is no time to slow down. But you have to find the time. Why? Because you have to slow down to get to where you want to be faster.

I took part in conducting a survey of over 500 employees and their managers in customer-facing industries like restaurants and retail. The survey solicited feedback from hourly employees just like yours, smack in the middle of the pandemic. We were trying to gauge the source of turnover and to understand why people were resigning. We assumed the common answer would be that employees who were leaving were offered better pay somewhere else. But the feedback we received was far more telling.

We learned that people didn't leave because of money, and they didn't stay because of it either. The pay difference between their current and new pay rates was marginal. Their current pay was competitive, and the difference was easily matched. No, the dollar amount was not the reason they were leaving. They left because there was nothing else keeping them at their current jobs. They didn't feel valued, they didn't feel important, they didn't feel included, and they didn't feel seen.

Indeed, they were treated much like I was treating my team when I was fixing my store after a long maternity leave: just like numbers. The money kept them there just long enough for them to find something else where they did feel appreciated and valued. And the hiring market was so competitive at that time that they found those opportunities quickly.

Among those who chose to stay and intended to stay, there was a common theme. They all described their managers as approachable and willing to work with them in the following ways:

1. Their managers allowed them the ability to take time to tend to life outside of work.
2. They felt comfortable approaching their managers with questions or mistakes.
3. Their managers listened to them and tried to resolve their obstacles to peak performance.

When your team members have problems, concerns, or issues outside of work that distract them, taking a moment to listen and respond to them is vital. Yes, taking that time also slows you down, and if you are rushing around, the pause can become annoying. We naturally adopt negative thoughts about barriers to getting our priorities accomplished. But, as our survey showed, if you don't slow down enough to be able to interact with your team members as people and treat them as human beings, it will slow you down a lot more in the long run, especially today.

Slowing Down Is Good for Business (and for You).

When you are able to skip a beat, set aside time to take a deep breath or two, you restore your emotional balance and introduce an opportunity for objectivity. At this slower pace, you can quiet your thoughts and calm your emotions. As your emotional connection to the moment dissolves, an ability to clearly notice what is truly happening around you presents itself. The pause enables you to consider the facts objectively and completely in order to come to more sound resolutions and more effective plans. Your metrics, staff, and customers will all benefit from your ability to operate from this wiser and more objective place.

Adopting a slower pace will also give you more balance in the other areas of your life. You will feel less agitated when you leave work, you will be able to dedicate your full attention to your family and friends, you will be present and engaged at important life events, and you will be healthier for it.

All those benefits will lessen the consequences that going too fast for too long inevitably create. Working more thoughtfully means that we face fewer hurdles to jump and less resistance on our path to achieving our goals. We can proactively anticipate obstacles. We allow ourselves a chance to find opportunities to work smarter, not harder. To get to where we want to end up more quickly, we have to slow down periodically.

Critical Times Call for Slow and Deliberate Measures.

Just as there are times when it is important for you to go fast, there are times where it is essential to slow down. Understanding the proper timing of each mode is crucial. Most of your time as a leader should be spent doing all of the things that you are required to do to run your business, and, of course, they should be done with urgency. There are certain key points in time, however, when slowing down is a must.

For example, when you have a new employee whom you haven't gotten to know yet, that would be a good time to take a pause. During a new employee's first day or two on the job, and throughout the first 30–60 days of their employment, it is essential that you slow down and take some time to get to know the new member of your team.

Another example of a time when you need to pull back the reins is when something is going wrong and you need to get to the crux of the matter, or when something is going right and you want to figure out what that something is so you can reward and repeat.

It's also helpful to slow down when crossing paths with an employee whom you haven't quite figured out or whom you have noticed is acting differently in some way. Has this typically talkative employee recently become withdrawn and quiet? Has this employee drastically changed the way that they look or are they talking about things differently than they used to? Perhaps they were previously very positive and, all of a sudden, everything they say is negative or a complaint about something. Or is an employee who was once very reliable now calling out of work frequently and not hitting deadlines?

Slowing down will allow you to see your employees from a change of perspective, which will help you strategize about how to pull them back into being high-performing assets on your team.

Learn to Read the Slow-Down Signs.

It is common for employees to give us warning signs that something is wrong. Some might actually let you know that they aren't loving working for you, aren't engaged in the business, and are not operating at maximum potential, but some signs are more subtle. Truthfully, managers aren't typically trained to pick up on vague clues. So, in all fairness, if you aren't taught, you won't know. Seasoned managers watch for signs of potential downturn, indicating that it is time to slow down and take a closer look. Once you know what to look for, you'll begin to see those signs within the culture of your team, within the environment you are working in, and within yourself.

Let's look first at the telltale signs within the culture in the store. Watch for the following indicators:

+ Team members are bickering.
+ Communication, both professional conversation and chit-chat, is limited among the group.
+ Your employees aren't asking you questions or seeking insight.

+ Your team stops sharing their feedback with you. (Note: Their silence is commonly an indicator that something is off, implying that trouble is brewing, although no one has said anything about it yet. No news is typically not good news in a team environment.)
+ Your employees start missing work and calling out.

Next, notice if issues are arising within the environment. They will be most noticeable when performance lags. If you are wondering whether trouble is brewing, consider how you might answer these questions:

+ Are KPIs hitting standard? Are they improving or declining?
+ Are customers indicating they are happy, or are you finding yourself handling guest complaints?
+ Is the condition of your office or building kept up, or is it deteriorating?
+ Are your sales increasing or decreasing?
+ Are you profitable, or is your profitability declining?

Last but not least, start to listen to your intuition. There are times when the warning signs to slow down come directly from yourself. In these instances, it is time for some honest self-reflection to determine whether you are approaching burnout. Ask yourself the following:

+ Am I able to take uninterrupted time off from work?
+ Am I spending enough time with friends and family?

✦ Am I feeling agitated with any of my employees? Are they getting under my skin?

✦ Do I have employees who would benefit from some candid feedback that I have not yet been able to give to them?

✦ Am I hitting deadlines consistently?

✦ Do I feel overwhelmed or tired?

Beyond those indicators, another huge red flag is one that most managers shy away from or don't know how to productively address. Have you ever seen an employee react emotionally in a way that seems to be much bigger than the situation warrants? My team member Charisse did just that, teaching me a very big lesson in the process.

Charisse's Story

When an employee of mine, Charisse, checked her schedule and saw that her hours had been cut, she freaked out big time. The reduction of hours wasn't personal. Her availability had changed, which resulted in her getting fewer hours. But Charisse hadn't done the math. When she came in to check her schedule, she lost it.

Charisse began yelling, slamming things around, and making big and charged allegations of discrimination and unfair treatment. It turned out that she had been under a significant amount of stress outside of work and was trying to balance work, childcare, school, and paying her bills. Her emotional outburst was cause enough for me to slow down to understand and help her resolve the concern. I hadn't taken the time to explain to Charisse why her hours had changed—an oversight made in haste, which was clearly on me. Once Charisse understood what had happened, the storm passed.

In the moment, though, I learned a valuable lesson: my actions, as the leader, have intentional and unintentional consequences. Both are equally significant and impactful to my employees. Had I understood Charisse's personal situation, I might have been able to prevent the outburst that my scheduling had unintentionally caused. It was a mistake that I vowed to try my hardest to avoid making in the future.

Being Proactive versus Reactive.

Many times, the need to slow down comes in response to a concern, or worse, a catastrophe. You can, however, limit the need to slow down by taking steps to slow down proactively. This strategy is far more effective, and typically preferable, because it is not in response to sticky, emotional situations. Slowing down from a heightened emotional state can require more willpower and effort than simply slowing down periodically when things appear to be running smoothly. In fact, slowing down from time to time when you don't see a pressing need will help you prevent issues in the first place.

To slow down proactively, you need to make it a habit or daily practice. Like most managers regularly preach to their crews, you likely know that it takes a certain amount of time before repetitive behavior builds a new habit. The slow-down habit is no exception. Below are some suggestions for how to build this healthy habit.

First, consider the way you organize and execute your tasks and priorities, and integrate slowing down into that process. Are you a to-do lister? If so, put "slow down" on your to-do list. Do you rely on sticky notes? If so, put one on your computer that reminds you of the need to sometimes slow down. Are you a time-blocker? If you are, block 10–15 minutes every day to slow down when it is convenient for you to do so. It may even be helpful to set a phone alarm or Google Reminder.

When you sit in your office with the door closed all day, it tells your team that you don't have time for them and aren't interested in what they have going on. Unless something is truly a confidential matter, open your door and get out and interact with your team.

Stack Your Good Habits into a Daily Practice.

Another practice that I have personally found helpful is what I call habit-stacking, which is when you add a new habit to a habit that you already have. For example, if you work in a warehouse and you are doing quality-assurance inspections, maybe during that important task is a time for you to purposely take a moment to slow down. Or maybe it's something as basic as when you arrive at work. Instead of going directly to your desk and getting to work, maybe that's a good time to slow down, before the day gets pulled away from you. If you are in a customer-facing industry, like restaurants, retail, or hotels, key times to practice slowing down are before or after customer traffic peaks.

Whenever we start new habits, it can feel like they aren't working because we don't see an immediate effect at the beginning, and we tend to give up. But remember that habits take time to build, and it can take even more time to reap the benefits. To counteract habitual sabotage to my own progress, I use a couple of tactics to keep me on track with a new habit.

The first is to make a new habit "time-bound" as opposed to seeing results bound to an outcome. So, instead of basing a decision to continue a habit only on a perceived outcome, I will simply commit to implementing the new habit daily. I always commit to at least 30 days before I decide if I need to rethink a new habit.

Second, like most people, I sometimes feel like creating a new habit is daunting. On those days, I find it helpful to remind myself of the benefits the new habit will produce: a more engaged team, an easier time hitting metrics, a better work environment, less friction among the team, a more balanced life, more time with my friends/family. When I consider how impactful the results can be, I frequently become recommitted to implementing the new behaviors I am trying to make into a new habit.

Key Takeaways:

- There are times to move fast, and there are times to slow down.
- Knowing this timing is crucial to your success.
- You have to pay attention to the warning signs to know when it is time to slow down.
- Warning signs can come from the way your business is performing, how motivated your people are, your health, or the dynamic of your personal and family life.
- Acting proactively in response to the signs ensures that you will course correct before damage is done.

CHAPTER 3

Gaining Perspective

AS A MANAGER, your line of sight from the ground is limited. To have access to all the information you need, you have to extract yourself from the hustle and bustle and rise above the action. A bird's-eye view presents a more complete picture. You get an outlook with more information and a broader perspective. From a great height, you can identify the key facts with clarity and objectivity as a result of this little bit of distance.

More information increases our effectiveness as leaders because we can better confirm and verify what we initially believe to be true. When employees come to us with complaints, or when tension builds within the group, having more information gives us the ability to identify what is really going on—to separate fact from emotion, the necessary from the extra.

Having all the facts can also provide us with a barrier to our personal bias and give us a chance to see things through the eyes of the crew, or the customer, or our employer. With an unbiased perspective, you can see through a clear lens, unclouded by your personal feelings, which could otherwise compromise your logic.

In my industry, which is hospitality, we call this a hawk's-eye view because we can see the situation the same way that a hawk can spy the entire landscape and still spot a mouse from hundreds of feet away. A hawk's-eye view gives us the ability to scan the environment and reveal what is going on around us. With this more complete view, we can pull ourselves off of the ground, removing ourselves from any emotionally influenced hustle and bustle, and rise above the stress of the moments playing out in real time on the earth below.

Herbert's Story

I was once contacted by an employee, let's call him Herbert, who was very angry at his manager. Herbert was relatively new to the team. He had only been employed by the company for about a month. When we spoke, Herbert alleged that he had been treated poorly by his General Manager and had been intentionally scheduled outside of his availability to set him up for failure. As you can imagine, Herbert wasn't too happy about this at all.

He told me that he wasn't alone. According to Herbert, every employee in this location was frustrated with their General Manager, and they were all going to quit. He said that working for their manager was stressful and belittling. Herbert shared that the manager was constantly playing favorites, allowing some people to get away with not showing up for shifts while writing others up for calling out. Herbert said that the manager would make sarcastic remarks that were belittling, and if someone didn't come in to cover a shift on their day off, they would lose hours the next week. Concerningly,

Herbert seemed pretty credible because he provided exact dates to back up his allegations as well as the names of other employees who he said could corroborate his claims.

When I asked for the name of the manager, I was shocked.

The manager's name was Tommy, and I knew Tommy very well and liked him a lot. Tommy had been a part of our leadership team for a very long time. He was highly regarded by the executive leaders and had been loved by his staff for years. In fact, staff from surrounding locations used to request to transfer into Tommy's store just to work for him. He had a reputation for being upbeat, high energy, and an incredible trainer. Tommy never had staffing issues because he was always the person everyone wanted to work for. People enjoyed working on his team, and they worked hard to make him proud.

I could barely believe that the complaints I had been hearing from this employee were about Tommy. Granted, when this complaint came in, the entire industry was struggling with staffing. It was as if a plague had been cast over all things hiring and retention. I knew that Tommy's store was no exception, but the change in Tommy's behavior described by this employee seemed inconceivable. This just wasn't the Tommy we knew.

As I normally do when investigating a complaint of this kind, I spoke to all of the witnesses of Tommy's reported conduct, and to my disappointment, they substantiated every single one of Herbert's claims. I was now very, very concerned. I had to call Tommy.

I initially asked him how things were going. Tommy shared

that he was getting through and making the best of the situation. I knew his answer wasn't a complete or fully accurate account of what was really going on. So, as I usually do, I asked a few more questions, and then I came out with it.

"Tommy," I said, "I have spoken to quite a few of your employees lately, and they have raised a lot of concerns. They are telling me that they feel you are intentionally scheduling them for hours they can't work and threatening to write them up if they don't pick up shifts that they weren't scheduled for. What is going on?"

At this point, the truth started to pour out of poor Tommy. He admitted that he was writing a schedule outside of people's availability because their availability wasn't fitting what he needed from them to keep the doors open. The changes in their availability had become so frequent and widespread that he felt as though they were making them out of spite. Because of this suspicion, he didn't even consider their needs anymore when writing the schedule. His mentality became solely focused on the business needs; he would schedule his team when he needed them, like it or not, and if they didn't show up, they would be disciplined for it.

Tommy also admitted to threatening to write up employees who didn't pick up extra shifts. Out of pure desperation, he had felt like he had no choice but to intimidate people into coming to work.

But he wasn't consistent with disciplinary tactics. Sometimes he used them to flex his authority, and at other times he felt scared to hold the team to company expectations because he was afraid that if he did, they would quit, and then he wouldn't have anyone left to schedule. He admitted that on bad days, when callouts were high and the restaurant got slammed, he would be more aggressive about discipline than on other days.

Tommy also admitted to making sarcastic jokes. He didn't mean them to be insulting. Tommy was usually an upbeat person, but because staffing had been such a struggle for so long, and because Tommy was so burned out, his lively, upbeat personality had turned into one that relied heavily on negativity and sarcasm.

As disappointing as this truth was to hear, I knew that there was still a great manager in there somewhere. We just needed to bring the real Tommy back out. His perspective was gone, and he was so lost in the weeds that he was having trouble seeing that a lot of the personnel issues he was having were self-inflicted.

The Perspective Tommy Needed.

Tommy spent so much time focusing on plugging the holes of a sinking ship that he lost sight of the course. His view of the total state of the ship, his business, was incomplete; he was missing the full picture. Had he pulled to higher ground, where he could objectively scan the ship, he would have been able to pinpoint what was really going on. The truth was that the team was just as frustrated with Tommy as Tommy was with them.

I had to help Tommy take an honest inventory of what was at

the root of his frustrations. His business was floundering, and he was overwhelmed. He felt out of control, and he reacted emotionally. Because Tommy was so engulfed in the emotional tit for tat with his team, he lacked the objectivity to see what was right in front of him. His team was telling him what was going wrong and how he could fix it, but he didn't have the perspective to see it.

When Tommy's team told him that he was playing favorites, they were telling him he was not being fair in whom he chose to discipline and when. They wanted consistency, but he was too defensive to hear that message.

Tommy's team told him that they couldn't come in for certain shifts, and when he scheduled them anyway, without speaking to them about why or asking them to make exceptions, he sent a very clear message to them: he didn't care about what was going on in their lives and what they might need. They responded in kind, showing frustration and throwing insults back at him, but he was too blinded to see why.

When Tommy's team confronted him by telling him that they felt his threats to discipline them were personal, Tommy felt just as personally attacked and reacted with the need to defend himself. At first, the team was simply telling Tommy that they didn't like being threatened. After all, who would? Because Tommy wasn't able to decode the message that they were sending to him, a general perception of hostility began to swarm through the entire team, and before he knew it, the entire team was against him.

The team made their feelings of being singled out clear in how they responded to Tommy. But Tommy was too tired and frustrated by their returned hostility and he couldn't see the pattern of backlash from his team aligning with the inconsistencies of his practices.

If you are frustrated with something, don't feel like you need to respond in the moment. Most things can wait a bit. Resist hitting send on the pissed-off email. Instead, respond thoughtfully after your emotions simmer down a bit. Never underestimate the power of a cooldown period.

Gaining a neutral position with a more complete compilation of the facts was what gave Tommy the impartiality and clear mind that he needed to pull himself out of the mess and get back in control of the sinking ship. To help him do it, we had to get clear on the answers to some very specific questions. We first had to challenge Tommy's assumptions about what he knew and what he may not have known. Together, we used a series of questions to help separate him from the emotion of the situation so that he could find higher, more objective ground. These same questions can be applied to any scenario. They can help you to rise above the fray and gain the perspective you need to get out of your own way and learn what needs to be done to get your team back on track.

What do you know, and what do you not know?

When you're mired in the moment, it's easy to make snap judgments. Before you can make a sound management decision of any kind, you need to know what you know—and know what you don't. As managers, we are constantly faced with pushback, frustration, disengagement, and underperformance from our teams. It is only when we slow down and separate ourselves from the moment that we can gain a fuller perspective to understand what is driving others to act or react in a given way. Then we can anticipate how they might react in the future.

Having this information also enables us to strategize proactively, making it possible for us to develop plans that are more likely to produce the results they are intended to by understanding what is motivating (or demotivating) each individual on the team.

Knowing what you know, and knowing what you don't, will give you the confidence you need to successfully lead a group of people. You won't question yourself because you will know that you have made a fully thought-out decision. Imagine the peace you will feel after proactively strategizing damage control before it happens, preventing yourself from being caught off guard!

What do you see, and what do you not see?

The way that employees interact with you and others will often show you if they are motivated. A motivated employee will actively interact with other employees and with customers. They typically smile, show up in proper work attire, are attentive in conversation, and make eye contact. Overall, a motivated employee shows that they are happy to be there and are ready for the day. If enthusiasm is lacking or is occurring on some days but not on others, you're likely seeing a need to explore further.

What do you hear, and what do you not hear?

A motivated and high-performing team will actively ask questions and contribute to conversations in a meaningful way. But if the team has gone radio silent, that could be as bad a sign as a slew of complaints just filed with your HR department. Something is brewing, and you should take notice.

What do you feel, and what do you not feel?

Call it a sixth sense, a vibe, or intuition. You know what I am talking about. Sometimes we just know when things aren't right—when something is off, when the energy is low, when the mood has shifted. When you get that impression, don't ignore it and hope that it will go away on its own. It won't. There is work for you to do. The second and third steps of SPARK will teach you how to go deeper here. But for now, simply recognizing that something is off gives you the objectivity you need to rise above the fray.

What You Stand to Gain with Perspective.

Through asking and answering questions with Tommy, I helped him gain clarity. Where he had believed that his team simply didn't care about their jobs, he came to realize that the complaints he kept fielding were actually his team telling him that they did care and wanted something different. He became aware of how intentionally scheduling people outside of their availability clearly signaled that he didn't care. And he realized that dropping sarcastic hints periodically (and not celebrating great performance) instead of addressing underperformance directly and consistently created an environment that was hostile and uncomfortable.

It was only when Tommy had an unobstructed, objective view of the facts that he was able to take stock of what he might be able to do differently and how his current choices were having the opposite effect from what he needed. As a result of his newly acquired knowledge, Tommy implemented some much-needed tweaks to how he interacted with his team. He listened more intently, stayed aware of what the team said they needed, and, instead of criticizing, he tried to resolve. Sooner rather than later, the team was back on track, and Tommy was back to his previous upbeat self, free from the downward cycle of criticism and spite.

Accurate Perspective Requires Accurate Facts.

The more information you take in, the better your chances of having the relevant information. But, on the flip side, you also open the floodgates to let in information that might not be completely accurate or relevant. Oftentimes, the information we receive is directly from our employees, and it can be a bit biased or even blown out of proportion.

The old saying "leave it at the door" has been a management staple for decades. But it isn't realistic. "Leaving it at the door" implies that work always takes precedence over personal situations. This is problematic because employees are people with the same emotional sway all human beings can be influenced by. So, when we take in the information they share with us, we must distinguish between accuracy that might be spot on or slightly (or even completely) off base.

Employees' assumptions and perceptions are frequently unedited and woven into what they share with you. False assumptions can also affect how a person acts and the choices they make. So, when scanning your environment, it is essential to recognize the need to distinguish fact from bias. If you react to inaccurate information, you run the risk of making decisions that are based on a weak foundation. But if you dismiss true and relevant information, you run the risk of disregarding what is truly affecting your team, thereby inhibiting your team's trust in you.

Snap decisions made with limited or inaccurate information

can impact people in unintended ways, leading to distrust and feelings of being overlooked and unimportant. When a leader acts on a more complete list of facts, their team begins to trust them. Your team will begin to trust you when they see that you understand how your decisions might impact them. They will know you are looking out for them.

Ultimately, that balance is what everyone seeks in an employer—to be seen, heard, and supported. And step one in being that employer is to first ensure that you have all of the information and have distinguished fact from perception.

Just the Facts, Ma'am.

An employee once called me with a complaint about her manager. She said that he was harassing her and that it was uncomfortable for her to work with him. When I asked her what, exactly, he was doing, she said that he would say hi to her when she was sitting in her car. That wasn't something that, at face value, I would consider an act that would make someone uncomfortable. So, I asked a few more questions.

I asked why it bothered her so much. Was it something he did when he said hi? Was it the way that he said it?

She told me that what made her uncomfortable was that he wasn't invited over to her car to speak to her. Her answer seemed odd to me. After chatting with her a bit more, I was able to confirm that she was parked right outside the employee entrance door, in a location that every employee had to walk by to get into the building.

Her manager saying hi as he was walking past her car to enter the building didn't seem over the top or harassing in the slightest. But she sounded terrified on the phone, which told me she was profoundly rattled by something. Her voice was shaking and cracking. She had a hard time staying on topic or finishing her sentences. Something was bothering her, but what she said didn't add up.

After speaking to her a little more, I soon found out what was making her so uncomfortable. There had been a rumor that this manager, an older gentleman, had been terminated from his previous job for sexual harassment. To make matters worse, rumors that he was involved in trafficking minors were circulating around this small town. The allegations came at a time when other stories of sexual harassment were appearing on the news daily. It was also during a time when the political landscape was hyper-focused on child abduction. Those external elements combined with the rumors that had surfaced about this man's past created a very real fear in this employee. She and the rest of the team were close, so they all shared their fears with each other, and soon, with a snowball effect, the whole staff was terrified.

Rumors in a workplace operate like a virus that interacts with the host and produces a million trillion variants. In the case of this example, as the rumors were repeated over and over again, they became more and more dramatic and less and less grounded in any facts at all. No one could even remember where the stories had gotten started.

Happily for all, the stories about the manager were untrue. And he hadn't harassed anyone in the store. He had been entirely cordial and polite. But the amount of hysteria that had spiraled off those exaggerated rumors had caused the crew to view everything he did and said with an assumption that his intentions were sinister, that he was trying to deceive them—or worse, was planning to kidnap and sex traffic them.

The leadership team on the ground was so overwhelmed by the panic and stories they were hearing that they couldn't get an objective grip on the situation. They needed a broader view, separated out from the hysteria and rumors, to be able to identify what they knew and what they didn't know and find the truth. Acting on rumors could have been nothing short of disastrous.

At the end of the day, we were able to conclude that there was not any indication that the manager was involved in any type of trafficking scheme. Nor did he have a record of any type of illegal allegations at all.

We had concerns in telling our scared employee that her fears were unfounded, but the rumor had to be put to bed so that the team could refocus on business. The conversation took some prepping because we wanted to ensure that the employee felt safe, that she knew that we heard her concerns completely, and that she didn't feel bad about coming forward. Realistically, the meeting with her could have gone one of two ways: She could feel as though we didn't do enough to protect her and that she was still in danger; or she could feel like we heard her complaints completely, looked into every detail she shared with us, and were able to determine that we did not find a threat. We had to make sure the result was the latter.

To make sure she felt safe and protected, we shared with her how diligently we had looked into each one of her concerns, and we let her know all of the precautionary measures we had in place (like background checks) to ensure that the people we hired were responsible, law-abiding individuals. That approach made her feel safe and sure that we would react if there was something that would threaten her safety. Had we simply dismissed her claims, assuming she had no basis to feel afraid (which, in this case, she did not), she would have felt unheard and unprotected.

Because we took the route that we did, she continued to stay loyal to our brand and worked for us until she graduated from college and moved on to her career of choice.

A manager's job is to find the truth and make sound decisions based on that truth.

Managers are tasked with making decisions daily, and those decisions have to be good ones in order to be successful. For a decision to be the best one possible for the business and the team, it has to be based on facts—information that is relevant, accurate, precise, complete, reliable, and timely. Rising above the hustle and bustle gives you the view and perspective you need to identify what, exactly, you know and what you don't know.

The decisions a manager makes are important. They have impact—not just on the business, but also on those on their teams. For example, budget decisions can impact quotas and the number of hours people work. Deciding to promote somebody may impact one person in a positive way but others in negative ways. A decision about resolving a conflict might have an impact on working conditions. Deciding who might take the lead on a project has implications too. And the decision to let someone go has enormous consequences on an employee's whole life, not to mention reverberating throughout the team.

It is common for managers to have trouble differentiating between the true and the exaggerated. Everybody sees their side of the story a little too big and the other side of the story a little too small. We know that to make sound decisions, it is important to have all of the facts, but what are the facts? A hawk's-eye view lifts you up out of the emotion of the situation, and then it's easier to see where the truth lies, which is usually somewhere right in the middle. To separate the wheat from the chaff, consider the questions below to determine what you know and what you don't know before making a decision.

What do you know and what do you not know about:

- + the working environment?
- + the team member's strengths and opportunities?
- + confirmed actions that have been taken?
- + changes that have recently taken place?

What do you see and what do you not see about:

- + employee behavior?
- + policy adherence?

- + changes in physical attributes?
- + the state of the work environment?
- + employee hygiene?

What do you hear and what do you not hear about:

- + what your employees are talking about?
- + what your employees are saying about others?
- + how they are reacting to direction or assigned tasks?
- + complaints from employees?
- + complaints from customers?
- + feedback from your boss?
- + your team's input or silence?

What do you feel and what do you not feel about:

- + the general vibe within the team?
- + your patience these days?
- + workload?
- + your own and your team's drive to keep going?
- + your confidence in the future?

Asking yourself these questions will bring you clarity and help you flush out the factual from the embellished. Only when you zero in on the facts can you truly understand your starting point. With an honest inventory of where you are and what is going on around you, you finally have a grounded base from which you can begin to strategize about how you might navigate the current situation. You gain a positional advantage with an understanding of where you are now, and you create a complete line of sight to pinpoint where you need to focus next.

In addition, you have also gained scale. Because you have removed your emotion from the equation, you can view all the facts and see them for what they are. Once you are removed from the hustle and bustle and clear on the facts, your problems feel less urgent. They appear smaller and less significant. You have provided yourself the space to think uninfluenced by stress, urgency, and the need for speed. It is now time to identify where you should focus your attention so that you can zoom back in as needed.

Key Takeaways:

- Line of sight from the ground is always limited.
- You have to seek higher ground to gain a complete and objective picture of the facts.
- The decisions a manager makes are based on the information they have, and these decisions have an impact on the team.
- When a manager acts on true facts, they gain trust and build momentum.
- To begin to build a motivated team, you first have to have all the relevant information.

Step 1 on a Page

The first step to motivating your team is to Slow Down to Gain Perspective.

Control the never-ending need for speed that forces managers to constantly try to get more done faster.

Productivity is great, but watch for burnout.

The focus on speed creates blinders and puts a divide between you and your team.

Speed also creates tunnel vision. Going too fast will cause you to miss important details.

If you are spending all of your time trying to get more done in less time, you will miss clues to what matters to your people.

If you want to motivate your team, you have to find out what makes them tick and connect work to those aspirations.

The clues to finding what matters to someone can only be seen when you have the full picture.

You have to find ways to pull yourself out of the hustle and bustle so you can do a complete scan and take in all the information you need to know; so first, slow down so you can seek higher ground with a complete view.

Step 2:

Pay Attention

IT'S EASY TO confuse listening and observing with paying attention. Hearing words and seeing symptomatic signs is not equivalent to understanding what is at the root of what is being said. Many times, people communicate what is on the surface, leading with emotion and fear. But the cause of their emotion and fear is what is most important for managers to uncover. It's what is driving their emotional response in the first place. Seeing and understanding a root cause enables us to resolve the real issue behind complaints and understand what truly SPARKs someone's will to work. That motivation is different for everyone. It is a personal thing, so to identify that core SPARK in each person, we need to pay attention to each of our employees in order to understand them as individual people.

What also tends to happen when we hear but don't truly listen is that we quickly think that we know where thoughts are coming from or that we know why people are saying what they do. Often, we assume that since we have done a person's job before, we know their circumstance and what they are up against. Or, even worse, sometimes we quickly conclude that someone is just being difficult, and we write off what they are saying altogether, giving little weight to their reason for being difficult because their behavior is an inconvenience or is distracting.

The truth is that we seldom know the true reason behind what people think, what they feel, or what makes them tick. But in order for a manager to build a motivated and high-performing team, that knowledge is essential.

Once we have perched on objective land and have scanned the full picture, we are positioned to identify clues to what these individually important things are. In the moment, however, it can be hard to figure out what might be clues and what might just be extra noise. We have to pay attention to the right clues because, if we tune in to the wrong thing and make assumptions about what is important to people based on what we believe or observe on the surface, we might run the risk of trying to connect to something that holds no weight or value. That outcome would be a disappointing waste of time. So, to ensure that you get this balance right, you need a strategic approach to focus your efforts and energy where they are best spent.

The second step of SPARK, Pay Attention, helps you to get clear on what exactly you should be paying attention to. This step will help you clarify what to tune in to as a potential clue and what to dismiss. If followed, this step will ensure that you are tuned in to the right clues. Without a blueprint to follow that shows you exactly how to identify what motivates someone, you will wind up spending more time than necessary in this Pay Attention phase. And, as we know, time is of the essence, so we have to use it wisely.

By executing the Pay Attention step, you will maximize every second that you spend scanning your environment with a clear understanding of what you are looking for. Here, you will learn to identify what might be the start of a trail of breadcrumbs that will lead you to accurately uncover a person's driver.

Making sure you scan accurately and efficiently requires paying closer attention than we typically do to clues large and small. In contrast to simply noting words or actions, paying attention requires us to patiently observe, acting more like a funnel, taking in the relevant information and screening out the irrelevant.

To successfully pay attention is to be sufficiently present with a person or in a situation, observing and noting all the information presented. The goal is to take in as much relevant information as possible about the person speaking. As you begin to take in more and more information about what someone's interests and goals are, you get to know them better. Make use of that very powerful tool because the connection creates a feeling of safety in both parties. Showing that you see, hear, and understand someone establishes support for their priorities.

The better you know your team, the better you will also be able to anticipate their needs. As projects and opportunities present themselves, you can better anticipate how your staff will be affected or what support they might want. Being able to proactively determine this can lead to better planning. It can also help you to react in a way that bypasses significant conflict and resistance within the team. Instead of ending up with chaos, you gain the ability to consider in advance how to leverage employee drive and strategically weave their motivations into planning and processes. But the only way to maintain the frictionless calm is to know what to pay attention to.

CHAPTER 4

Paying Attention Means More than Just Staying Alert

PAYING ATTENTION TO collect the relevant information needed to exercise sound and fair judgment is a critical component in building and managing a high-performance team. This kind of attention ensures that you will have a comprehensive understanding of the factors that impact both your employee(s) and your business. And it isn't as easy as it looks! It requires enormous concentration and an ongoing awareness of—and sensitivity toward—your whole staff. It's challenging, nuanced, and complex. Mastering this technique, though, will ensure that your information is as current and accurate as possible so that your communication and planning are impactful and helpful.

Having the relevant information also helps you reduce the risk of suddenly waking up to a disengaged, underproductive team. Instead, you are positioned to use the information to build a highly productive, motivated group of supported and engaged employees or to pull a team out of the fire. Miss the early warning cues, and by the time you call in the fire department, it may be too late.

Molly's Story

Molly was a strong district manager whose results captured the attention of all of the corporate execs. Not only did she lead her market in metrics, but you could frequently find her name on the list of the top 10 performers in the company that circulated monthly. Her name was frequently brought up as a top talent with a high potential for advancement. Molly was being watched for potential growth opportunities. The company had high hopes for her, and she was excited about that.

As great as Molly's metrics were, she wasn't perfect. There were times when her team's results would waver. But what made Molly so great is that she could coach each person on her team back into performing at the level they had before. She seemed to do this effortlessly. But then, oddly enough, Molly's momentum shifted. Almost overnight, she started losing her people at record rates. One by one, they resigned or just stopped showing up.

As one might expect would happen when someone was losing their seasoned people, Molly's results started to suffer. Things got so bad that you could no longer find Molly's name in the all-star section of the company circular. In fact, Molly's name quickly began to drop to the bottom, and she was now being noticed for all the wrong reasons. It was clear that, for some reason, Molly had lost her mojo.

Along with every other bottom performer in the company, Molly now had to start to attend the dreaded "bottom performer conference call" regularly. The call forced leaders to share publicly what they weren't doing well and to be pre-scribed a plan to fix their problems. The discussion was about 10% sharing and 90% being "spoken to" by company executives like me who were tasked with getting her back on target.

Having to attend these calls was embarrassing, especially for someone who was normally a high achiever like Molly. She held conference calls with her GMs regularly. Her calls used to be upbeat. The GMs would celebrate their wins, and they would brainstorm ways to become even better. The posi-tive momentum had been infectious—but not anymore. As results slipped and Molly had to attend more "bottom per-former" calls, her team chats started mirroring the negative tones from those calls.

Now Molly's team calls were mostly focused on calling out her team's bad results and everything her leaders were doing wrong. I remember attending a call where Molly asked one of her GMs to speak to their own results. "So, I see that your results here are at the bottom of the district, again, for the fourth week in a row. How, exactly, are you going to fix this?" she demanded, sounding very annoyed.

No one wants to sit and listen to you talk for 20, 30, 60 minutes at a time. For a team call (or team chat, for that matter) to be productive and leave all feeling inspired, get the individual(s) involved in the process of improvement. Ask for regular updates on their results, ask them what is going well, ask them what support they need.

The GM answered as humbly as he could but called me as soon as the call ended. He said that he was upset that Molly had spoken down to him on a call with his peers listening. He felt belittled. He also shared that he and many of his fellow GMs had put feelers out for new jobs. They were sick of getting beaten up on calls and felt like no matter what they did, Molly would never be happy.

Later that month, I talked to Molly about a complaint that had come in through our hotline about one of her stores. When I called her, she was driving to another one of her locations. As we were chatting about the claim, Molly pulled into the parking lot and noticed one of her managers out front, smoking. "See, see," she said. "This is what I am dealing with!" she yelled. "Now I have to write him up too! What is wrong with everyone?"

On my end, I had no idea what she was talking about at the time. I couldn't see what was going on. All I heard was her yelling at me.

"Molly," I said in an even tone designed to calm her down (and, by this point, calm myself down too). "Pull out of the parking lot and go to a different store. Let's chat about this tomorrow." I began to see that the negative reports from Molly's staff were based in some reality.

The manager who had been out front smoking had broken policy, and he knew it. He had been with the company for a very long time and had never been blatantly dismissive of the rules before. Something had changed, so I called that manager later that day to find out what it was.

"I don't see the point in trying anymore," he told me. "Every time Molly is in the store, she tells us how everything we do is wrong. She's always in a bad mood and on a hunt to find everything we aren't doing right. I know I am not perfect, but what is the point in trying if all she is going to do is beat us up anyway?"

The next day, I called Molly back. This time, though, I called her first thing in the morning, before her team even had a chance to make errors that would surely stress her out. We talked for almost an hour. I brought up the incident with the manager smoking and asked her why she thought he had made such a seemingly careless choice. She went on a rant about how she didn't know why he had done that, and she couldn't figure out why all of her other managers just didn't seem to care either. She listed problem after problem with each of her people and how she saw no other option but to just "write them up."

"Molly," I asked her, "do you think that there might be something going on here that you aren't completely aware of?"

Her reaction was clear annoyance. "Well, of course there is! But if I knew what that was, I wouldn't have this problem!"

I had anticipated a response along those lines, so I simply asked her what she had done to figure it out. She listed all the things she had done: walk-throughs, calls, reminder emails, written warnings. You name it, she had done it. Then, I asked her something that stopped her in her tracks.

"Molly," I said, "you have listed all the things a manager would do to identify things that are wrong with their team's work.

But what about *them*?" Confused by my question, she simply repeated everything that she had just said: walk-throughs, calls, emails, warnings, etc.

I asked Molly how her calls were going. She said that they were long, but they had to be because so much was going wrong. I then asked her how participation was on the calls.

"Participation? What do you mean?" she asked.

"How engaged are they with the topic on your calls? Do they contribute? Do they ask questions? Do they share what they are doing?"

After some back-and-forth, Molly finally admitted that her team didn't contribute at all on calls. I asked her how they interacted with her after her calls. She admitted that they were distant, avoided her calls, or were short with her on the phone. I then asked how results were after her calls. Did they get better or worse, or did they stay the same? She said that they either stayed the same or got worse.

"I see," I said. "Do you think that maybe your team is telling you something even without verbally telling you what is going on?"

"What does that even mean?" she asked me.

"Molly, what that means is that they are telling you that the approach you are taking is making them not want to try any-more. Right now, you are so focused on catching everything that is wrong and correcting them on it. Everything you say to them is a criticism. Isn't there anything they are doing right? Do you know why the things that are going wrong are going wrong? If all you focus on is the negative, how can you expect positive results? If you want them to start caring again, you are going to have to change your approach," I told her.

Although she resisted me at first, Molly eventually came around. Once she started paying attention to the signs that her team was showing her, she was able to identify the things that were happening within her team. Some were newer in their roles and simply didn't have the knowledge or skill sets they needed to be successful, so she trained them better. She learned that some had been working for over 10 days straight and hadn't seen their families for more than five minutes in passing in weeks. These people needed time to recover and be with their loved ones. Others had spouses who had been laid off during a recent economic downturn and were struggling to adjust to one income. Each scenario created significant stress and disengagement at work.

Having this information about her people enabled Molly to tweak her approach to keep her team motivated and working toward filling the voids that were in their lives while simultaneously accomplishing their goals—and hers.

Objectivity is paramount when paying attention.

When we take in information and filter it through our assumptions, the integrity of the data becomes compromised. Only by receiving information in an unfiltered way are we able to see the facts completely and accurately. Cutting corners in seeking this information will be detrimental to the motivation of your team.

Assumptions, preconceived ideas, and misconceptions are the Achilles heels of objective attention and judgment. It's easy to fall into the trap of assuming you have all the information or that you know why employees are acting the way that they are. My many years of experience supporting managers and their teams have confirmed for me that most of the time, even though managers think they know things, they really don't. Or what they know is, at best, only a piece of the pie.

What we believe to be the objective truth is often an incomplete picture, shaded by our assumptions, resulting in decisions and actions that can negatively impact the team's morale. Assumptions work to keep you stuck in the past; they don't support growth into the future.

As managers, we tend to lean on assumptions because they make us feel safe and in control. They are also quicker to the punch than more considered opinions might be. Back to that need for speed!

Assumptions let us hide behind our version of a story, our perspective, which gives us the illusion that we know everything. While operating in this state might make us feel better, it can also be the cause of unnecessary stress and can contribute to unmotivated teams.

For example, you might assume that someone not showing up for work was the result of them not caring, but the true cause might be something that was outside of their control. Or you might write off an employee with a terrible attitude as just "difficult," but the reality could be that they feel underacknowledged and taken advantage of at work.

Disconnect Your Trip Wires.

We can do a few things to hack into your assumptions and disconnect your managerial trip wires to make sure they don't fire off whenever you have to make a decision. The most important step here is to make sure that you remain emotionally neutral. Slowing down and standing back from a situation helps you to accomplish this. But your attention is called to the next level of awareness, which you can achieve by following these steps:

1. Ask yourself about whom or what the situation is that you are confronting. Hint: The actual problem is almost never about you. Even if an employee is upset and blames you for something, and they often will, don't take it personally. What they are upset about is how the situation affects them and their life, and it is completely about them. Maintaining a rational mindset will help you refrain from getting your feelings hurt or fighting the wrong battles with an employee. It will create a barrier between their emotion and your response, protecting you from reacting with an equal amount of unproductive emotion. This approach will help you stay focused and able to objectively understand their point of view.

2. Resist the urge to justify or explain yourself. When you jump in with an explanation or a defensive justification, it sends the message that you aren't hearing what your

employee is saying and that you don't take them seriously. Instead, simply listen and take note of their words and feelings. Think of questions you may wish to ask later and jot them down. Writing things down when they occur to you is better than saying them without thinking and creates an immediate emotional buffer against whatever you are feeling in the moment.

3. Later, think carefully about what you might ask them in order to clarify what you heard. Word your questions to reflect that you are trying to learn more about them as a person. That step will help you to limit any bias or assumption that might unintentionally creep in.

4. Actively search for what I call the X factor—that one missing piece of information that might make the whole situation suddenly clear. Taking this approach will not only help you to remove yourself from the equation but will also help you understand why your employee is approaching you with something or behaving in a way you don't understand. Those pieces of information serve as clues to what might be underlying a complaint or concern.

Key Takeaways:

- You have to know what you are looking for to get the facts.
- You have to look for clues about what the individual(s) find important.
- Objectivity is essential to uncovering the truth about their values and SPARK.
- Know that you will naturally want to jump to conclusions when gathering facts. Resist that temptation.
- Your first conclusions are seldom completely accurate, so listen objectively longer.

CHAPTER 5

How to Look for the Clues

HUNTING FOR CLUES is a powerful managerial tool that's frequently underutilized. A clue serves as an indicator to what is going on beneath the surface. Thinking of it like a good old-fashioned treasure hunt where you find clues that gradually reveal the whole truth is a great approach to management. Clues can reveal what is most important to your people, the true state of your team, the driving cause behind the culture within your business, and the direction in which your team is heading. To home in on the clues, it is helpful to operate with this thought in mind:

> ***What is your employee revealing
> about what is important to them?***

This mindset is the secret to unlocking your team's motivation and drive. Just like in an actual treasure hunt, you can find clues in all sorts of places. Here are a few important kinds.

Visual Clues.

People surround themselves with the things that matter the most to them. Fashion, jewelry, photos, hairstyles, even key chains can tell you a lot about somebody. For example, people will frequently carry pictures of places, people, or things that bring them joy, such as family, friends, memories, life experiences, or adventures. Avid sports fans will frequently wear their sport team's logo. Some are even so dedicated to a person or concept that they will have a visual reminder of that thing permanently branded on their bodies with tattoos. All are important clues that can begin to tell you a lot about the person you are working with.

A Picture Is Worth a Thousand Words.

+ Danny's desk has a framed picture of him and his army buddies at the top of Mount Everest. Danny is an avid mountain climber, and it is a passion that he developed with his army buddies after returning from deployment. His connection to his unit is strong, and they are a massive support to him after their return from Afghanistan.
+ Terry has a keychain with a photo of her son in a baseball uniform. Her son is only 14, plays on a highly competitive baseball tournament team, and travels all over the U.S. competing with the top 10 teams in the country. This level of baseball takes considerable commitment, and every second of Terry's life outside of work is spent schlepping her son to baseball lessons, practices, or multiple doubleheaders a weekend. Sometimes she even takes work with her to practices to make sure her son doesn't miss them. All of Terry's vacation time is reserved for attending national tournaments out of state. She dedicates her free time to supporting her son's dream, and she wouldn't have it any other way.

+ Nick arrives at work every day in a Colts sweatshirt. He is a huge fan. Nick never made it to the NFL, but he did play D1 football in college. Nick knows the game inside and out and is passionate about the sport. The dedication to football also runs in the family. His youngest brother is also a D1 player and is currently being scouted by the NFL. The entire family is ecstatic about this.

+ Erica recently earned a business degree. She took classes part-time for six years so that she could balance work and school. Erica had to pay her way through college and was the first in her family to earn a degree. She has recently proudly displayed the framed diploma on her office wall.

Every one of your employees has something—a story, an experience, or a passion—that sparks a fire within them, and visual clues can help you start to get a handle on what those things are. Even talking about these things, just for a moment, can ignite positivity and motivation within your employees. Acknowledging their interests also lets them know that you see them and that you care about the things that are important to them. That feeling of connection and being cared about is more precious than gold.

Audible Clues.

Positive or negative, people talk about what's important to them. If they are excited about an event or an idea, you won't be able to get them to stop talking about it! Similarly, when something upsets them, when something they value—self-esteem, their time with their child(ren)—is threatened, they will probably say something about that too. Tuning in from time to time to take your team's temperature and pick up on everybody's verbal clues will give you invaluable insight into the health and well-being of your whole culture.

Tune In to Their Life.

+ Allison came into work the other day five minutes later than usual and in a terrible mood. As soon as she came in, she went straight to the coffee machine. While pouring her coffee, she was chatting with a coworker about how terrible the drop-off line was at her child's elementary school. It was the beginning of the school year, and Allison's child was entering first grade.

+ Larry is a full-time nurse. Recently, his cousin started a vegan diet and has experienced incredible relief in body aches and joint pains. Not only did his cousin have less pain, but his energy was on a totally different level. Larry noticed that his cousin could work out like he could 10 years before. The noticeable improvement was inspiring to Larry, especially because getting older was starting to take a toll on him too. After years of working on his feet, Larry had begun to develop back problems. He decided to start a plant-based diet to see if it might help him like it had helped his cousin. He has been sharing interesting medical facts with his coworkers about the benefits of eating plant-based foods.

+ Phillip is an aspiring leader. He has been with the company for four years and has been doing very well in his role. He speaks up regularly in team meetings and makes suggestions on new projects and endeavors. Phillip has excellent ideas, and it is clear that he is a big thinker capable of growth within his job.

+ Arnold has become bitter. He is always complaining about the company's new operating procedures and the way the company is changing. He liked things better the old way. The biggest obstacle for Arnold is that he is not comfortable with technology, and all new initiatives are embracing technology more and more. Although he has a smartphone and is in the millennial age group, he doesn't really fit the typical millennial persona because he grew up without computers and the internet in his household. No one ever taught him how to use the technology, so he isn't comfortable with it. The technological shift in company processes is making him feel like he is failing at his job.

Managers Can't Depend on the Grapevine.

Some of my managers avoid talking to their teams about topics that aren't work-related or that don't personally interest them. Don't miss this huge opportunity! Even though I might not be interested in mountain climbing or I am not a football fan, what is important is that my employees are. My interest, as a leader, should always be to understand what is important to my employees because that is what SPARKs a fire within them; it is where their motivation is hiding. No matter how unrelated to work an employee's interests might seem, we can connect that SPARK to our work simply by showing curiosity about what they are talking about. So, it is important to always stay tuned in to their lives.

In fear of getting sucked into gossip or validating rumors, many managers also tend to shy away from understanding what their teams are discussing when they are unhappy about something. Thinking that avoiding such conversations is a wise choice couldn't be further from the truth. Of course, getting involved in and contributing to gossip is not helpful. But listening to and understanding what your team might be discussing can unveil something that needs to be addressed. When left unattended and uncontrolled, chatter in the workplace can derail productivity and progress. Staying in tune with the watercooler talk will help you stay connected to what the team is happy with and what pain points might need your attention.

Sometimes silence speaks louder than words. Not communicating is also a clue. People typically retreat into silence for one of two reasons: either they feel overpowered and therefore don't see the point in sharing, or they feel that something that they hold close to them is in some way threatened. Going silent is a clear indicator that something is wrong and signals that they are disengaging from the work you need them to be energetically engaged in.

If an employee makes a suggestion, there is a reason they are bringing it to your attention. Something about that suggestion will affect them in a way that matters to them. So don't dismiss suggestions. Listen, consider them, and determine if they are feasible. If the answer is yes and you can make what they're asking for happen, do it.

When someone gets angry, reacting emotionally, usually in a bigger way than a situation would warrant, that also gives us a clue. People respond emotionally when they feel wronged or are afraid of being hurt. It is a defense mechanism that notifies us that they feel as though we, or the business, are a threat to them or something they care deeply about. When such incidents happen, it is essential to separate your own emotion from their behavior and instead to seek to understand what they feel a need to protect because that thing means something to them.

Honor Your Team's Personal Priorities.

Managers also tend to shy away from learning about what their employees do in their off time. We figure if it isn't work-related, it isn't any of our business. Although joining in on their off-time activities probably isn't appropriate for managers, dismissing an opportunity to learn what your people do when they are not at work is a missed chance to identify their true passion and drive. So ask yourself if you know what your people do in their off time. Do they have hobbies? Do they play a sport? How do they spend their weekends?

That knowledge is extremely important for managers because people make the time for the things and people that they love. Spending time doing what they love brings joy. If working for you limits their ability to spend the time doing what they are passionate about, what lights them up, they will begin to resent working for you. Instead of having a motivated employee, you will have one who drags down the vibe and all the other employees along with them.

Just how impactful this internal drive is to the workplace was magnified by the COVID-19 pandemic. Throughout 2020 and 2021, allowing work leniencies became a necessity, not a luxury. The entire globe was put on virtual lockdown. We were unable to interact in person with loved ones or to venture out to do the things we were passionate about. Losing those freedoms highlighted just how important they were to us.

Before the pandemic, we used to consider pushing off things like family gatherings, important connections, self-care, and our own well-being in order to put in a little extra work on that important project or to get noticed by that C-suite executive.

People are now saying no when asked to sacrifice time doing what they love and are instead protecting that time for what they now prioritize. In fact, in many industries, like the hospitality industry, where we often feel a pressure to sacrifice priorities, people are simply walking away. In 2021 over 47 million people voluntarily left their jobs. This is taken from the bureau of labor statistics: https://data.bls.gov/pdq/SurveyOutputServlet. Why?

Because the jobs that they were in no longer met their needs. They found better options.

For example, some people left for flexible scheduling in order to balance a work schedule and childcare. In some industries, flexible scheduling was nearly impossible. Those employees felt forced to look elsewhere. In the study that I conducted, one of the top reasons employees shared about why they chose to stay with their employers was that their managers were able to accommodate their personal scheduling needs.

But the reasons weren't only for childcare or school. An article in the *New York Times* highlighted how working remotely has enabled some employees to save a nest egg that they weren't able to previously. Others have shared how remote working has allowed them to save time and money by not traveling into work, which has created a better quality of life for them. They have replaced commuting time with activities that are enjoyable and good for them, such as spending time at the gym.[1]

The magnitude of people leaving jobs that don't support their priorities is evidence that people will act to preserve their ability to protect their personal time. That perspective is important for managers to adopt and understand when choosing how to lead. Acknowledging how your employees spend their time outside of work—and protecting their ability to do those things—is

---

1   Maria Cramer and Mihir Zaveri, "What if You Don't Want to Go Back to the Office?" New York Times, May 5, 2020, https://www.nytimes.com/2020/05/05/business/pandemic-work-from-home-coronavirus.html.

paramount not only in maintaining their drive, but also in retaining them in general.

Develop your sixth sense and pick up on extrasensory clues.

When things feel awkward or uncomfortable, a good manager is sensitive to the shifts in the cultural vibe. Extrasensory clues, otherwise known as reading the room, will typically alert you if things are going well or if something is wrong.

Stepping into work and seeing your team engaging with one another, smiling, and saying hi to you and others is usually an indication that all is well. If such observations are paired with great conversation at meetings with open participation and feedback, quality work coming from your team, and fantastic reviews shared by your customers, chances are that things are probably going pretty well on your team.

In contrast, if you find yourself observing silence, team members isolating themselves, or chatter stopping when you or someone else walks into the room, you need to pay closer attention. An atmosphere like that can quickly start to affect results. Deadlines might be missed, work might be rushed, and customers might start to complain. If the team vibe is off and your gut is telling you something is wrong, chances are your intuition is right.

Candy's Story

Sometimes bad vibes aren't indicative of the state of the team, but instead are unique to an individual. I remember Candy's story distinctly. She was in sales, a top producer. Candy had won awards for top salesperson of the year and had been recognized at annual conferences, awarded with cruises and lavish trips for her and her family to attend, compliments of the CEO. Over time, though, her performance began to decline, and one day her boss looked at her results and was confused at what she saw. Candy's midyear reports were barely trending at the company average. Not only were her results dropping, but her demeanor had changed. She barely smiled anymore, and it seemed like she resented having to drag herself to work every day. Her emails shifted from being upbeat and optimistic to short and curt. She started complaining about clients and got angry at subdepartments for not following through on what the customer was expecting. There was an obvious change in Candy, and it was a clear indication that something was very wrong.

It turned out that a few months earlier, when the company had changed the comp structure, it had significantly limited Candy's earning capacity. Candy worked to make money. She didn't care much about connections at work. She had an incredible group of friends and a supportive family outside of work. She also didn't care much about titles or upward mobility. She saw climbing the ladder as steps toward more responsibility and less control over her earning capacity. Candy saw the time that she spent at work as a personal investment because it was time that she wasn't spending with her family, her priority.

When the comp structure changed, she lost her drive. Her reason for working was taken from her, and she was bitter about not being able to make the money she wanted to make. So, she stopped sacrificing time with her family to produce for the team.

In the end, Candy chose to leave that pay structure for another sales job that gave her the earning capacity she had previously enjoyed. Her old employer lost a top producer, and her new employer gained a rock star.

What to Do with the Clues You Uncover.

Finding the clues to what might be holding an unmotivated employee back is an enormous breakthrough, but it is just the beginning. There is still work to be done. Now that you have identified your focus point and locked in on the subject, it is time to zoom back in.

The Inscrutable Tale of a Boy and His Earbuds.

I supported a store in the Northeast with an employee who was constantly putting earbuds in every chance he got. It was nearly impossible to get him to take them out, and it was even harder to get him to keep them out. A manager would ask him to put them away, and after 15 minutes, he would put them right back in. We would frequently find him in the back of the building with those earbuds having magically reappeared in his ears. If taking out the trash was his responsibility that day, it would take him a particularly long time to empty the cans because he would be standing out by the dumpster listening to whatever was blasting in his ears.

Most of the managers had written him off as challenging, insubordinate, and unproductive because of what they saw on the surface: a lack of urgency to complete tasks, an inability to follow direction, and a general disengagement from the team. Many had tagged him as lazy and unmotivated. He was also frequently late and would mosey on in at a snail's pace, even if the team was getting slammed.

I could have landed on the same conclusion as every other manager. But instead of taking the traditional approach of "holding him accountable" and managing him out, I chose to recognize that he may have a valid reason for his behavior.

One day I brought up how frequently he used his headphones at work, and instead of reminding him of the policy, I changed it up. I asked him what he was listening to. I genuinely wanted to know. I suspected that it must be something good since he kept gravitating back to wearing them.

Simply asking this question unlocked so much information about this young man and what he was looking to accomplish in life. It turns out that he was an artist—actually, a musician—and he was trying to break into the music scene. He had composed his own music and was listening to it over and over again to critique it. He was constantly rethinking how to improve it. He would listen to the same phrase over a hundred times to perfect it.

Think about the amount of dedication and commitment it takes to listen to the same notes over and over and over again—and to be pulled back to that thing over and over again, even if you were told not to listen to it. If that isn't motivation, I don't know what is. You see, this guy, whom most wrote off as uninterested, lazy, and unmotivated to do anything, was the most dedicated and motivated person on the team, far more than even me. The problem was that his motivation just wasn't connected to the work we were asking him to do.

After some more conversation about his music and what he had been able to accomplish in the music scene, the rest of the team and I became completely engulfed in learning more. He started coming to work with frequent updates about his music journey, and his outside passion became a regular topic of conversation with the entire team. At one point, he spoke about his music with the team so often that he even stopped listening to it while at work. Because he was interacting with the people on the team and talking throughout the shift, he was far more engaged in the work and became much more productive as an employee.

Was leadership ever in his future? Probably not. And that's okay. Not all of our employees want to go into leadership. Their goals not aligning to career advancement don't automatically make them low performers. Yet we still need them to perform well in their jobs. My headphones junkie was smart and could have done well at the store if he chose to, but leadership wasn't in his future because he saw a different path for himself. Even though he wasn't interested in growing with the company, he became engaged and productive because work surrounded him with people who took interest in his craft and supported his dream.

Now he worked with a group of people who saw and accepted him for who he was and what he was passionate about, so he showed up for shifts on time. He would spend his shifts in a good mood and smiling with coworkers and customers. And he began to contribute to what we were all working toward. After all, we cared about what mattered to him, and he felt compelled to return the favor.

Suddenly, our once withdrawn and uncaring employee blossomed into an engaged, motivated, and productive one. His coworkers became a source of support and encouragement while he was paving his way in the music scene. While our restaurant certainly wasn't going to get him a record deal, we could still connect the work to what mattered most to him by becoming his biggest fans.

Key Takeaways:

- Clues present themselves in many forms. You just need to know where to look.
- Visual: People surround themselves with things that are important to them.
- Audible: People talk about the things that matter to them.
- Time: People make time for the things that bring them joy and hold value.
- Extrasensory: The vibe people give off will show you if they are passionate about something.

CHAPTER 6

Identifying The Message Behind The Message

IN A PERFECT textbook scenario where you are choosing to separate yourself from the hustle and bustle to give yourself some essential perspective, gaining objectivity is simple. Unfortunately, not every scenario that requires objectivity is a calm and controlled textbook environment. Sometimes, the clues to what matters most to someone present themselves in intense, reactive moments that can catch us off guard.

All managers will inevitably encounter emotional moments with employees where their response seems to outweigh the moment. Seemingly out of nowhere, they get extremely angry or defensive, and we don't see it coming. Maybe they interpreted something inaccurately, took something in a way you didn't mean, or responded to an event in a way that you didn't anticipate. Whatever the trigger, they became very upset and emotional as a result of it.

These bigger-than-anticipated moments can present themselves in a variety of ways. Some employees may start yelling, make passive aggressive comments, flash dirty looks, or make snarky remarks. The natural response to such moments is to react defensively. And from a human perspective, that reaction makes sense! Their actions can evoke feelings of embarrassment and make us feel defensive, out of control, challenged, or disrespected. In an attempt to regain control and respect, managers often make attempts to overpower the employee by talking louder than them or subconsciously stand taller and wider to attempt to take up more space (a natural response that enables them to nonverbally gain control and power). We may even feel the need to defend our actions or decisions by justifying what the employee is upset about. In the moment, we might feel that using defensive tactics will work to defuse the situation, but most of the time they just perpetuate it, launching a full-blown power struggle.

These reactions can have a lasting effect, both on you and on the team. After a power struggle, the rest of the team can feel uncomfortable around you or the upset employee. Or, even worse, they may side with the angry employee and turn against you and your leadership team.

It's only natural to meet an emotional outburst with more emotion because being the target of an emotional fit feels personal. We feel threatened, or even attacked. For hours or even days, we may hold a grudge and try to further convince ourselves that we were right and the other person was wrong. We may write off their response as overly sensitive and blown out of proportion. We might dismiss their behavior as overdramatic and a result of their ability to never be happy. Each of those responses make us feel better in the moment because it fools us into thinking that we were right.

I would challenge you to think differently. If you are so focused on being and proving that you are right, you will be limited in what you can achieve. Figuratively putting an employee in their place solely to regain the feeling of control sends them a very clear message: we simply don't care. While the truth is that their conduct is what you are attempting to control, they will read it as you dismissing what they are upset about. We are essentially telling them that whatever it is they are reacting to isn't important. That underlying message works to disengage the employee from you and the business, not to reengage them.

They speak the truth. Are you listening?

Getting lost in the emotional response wave fueled by defensiveness in an attempt to protect your authority is counterproductive to finding and lighting the motivational SPARK. Many managers don't realize the opportunity that exists in moments of emotional explosions. These types of scenarios, where both reaction and behavior are bigger than the moment warrants, can lead us to some of the most telling clues to what makes a person tick. Typically, the bigger the reaction, the more powerful the motivation behind the eruption.

With emotional reactions comes a message behind the message. The employee is revealing to us, nonverbally, that they feel as though they are at risk of losing something that means a lot to them. They might fear earning less money, which is essential for their survival; they might have already sacrificed important time with a loved one and be unwilling to sacrifice more; you may have inadvertently injured their ego by brushing over the effort they put into a project, and it hurt their pride; maybe your response landed in a way you didn't intend, and it hurt their self-esteem, making them feel bad about themselves.

To understand emotional responses more completely, take a moment to step into your employees' shoes. Consider how you might answer these questions:

+ What is it that means the most to you? Is it your family, your child(ren), your pride, your title, survival?
+ How would you feel if someone threatened to take any of those things away from you?
+ How would you react to that threat?
+ What emotions come up for you in this imaginary scenario?

The emotions revealed by your answers are the same emotions that your employees feel when they are reacting in a way that is bigger than the moment. But you are only seeing their reaction in the the third and fourth bullet points—the response to what they are perceiving as a threat. While your employee's response might seem to you to be over the top and unwarranted, it may be the clearest clue of all to what makes them tick. But to pick up on the clue, you have to be emotionally removed enough to maintain objectivity and gain perspective. So simmer down your natural response and remove the emotional blinders.

Removing the Emotional Blinders.

I had the privilege of working alongside a gifted and down-to-earth labor law attorney who shared a profound point that stayed with me for many years. Here was the lesson:

In the majority of employee relations complaints and lawsuits filed, the root cause is almost always a manager's failure to identify the message behind the message.

Had the managers been astute enough to hear the real problem—the issue fueling the intense moment—most conflicts and cases could have been cut off at the pass because the managers would have been able to address the root of the issue.

The most common examples that I see of these moments manifesting at work are:

+ A reduction of hours: Fewer work hours might make someone react angrily because the cut means less money, which impacts their ability to pay bills or to keep a roof over their own or their family's heads and food on the table.

+ Getting passed up for a promotion: Stagnating in a position can impact people's sense of self-worth and ignite a fear of not being valued.

+ A project getting canceled: A person might really be looking forward to a project because they see it as a chance to demonstrate a competency or skill set. Or, if a project meant allowing more of an opportunity to connect to their passions, such as travel or bringing them closer to family, it might make them feel disconnected and alone.

+ Not receiving recognition that they feel they have earned: When a person feels as though they have put in significant effort and have earned a level of recognition, not being recognized in the manner they believe they deserve can hurt their ego and trigger a fear of worthlessness.

+ Correction or coaching conversations: Sometimes people are very proud and believe that they don't need coaching. For these types, receiving feedback can be hard because correction can make them feel less than competent.

+ Not receiving a raise or receiving less of a raise than hoped for: Many equate money with self-worth and value. When they don't receive the bump in pay they are expecting, or as much as that of a colleague, it can frequently result in an assumption that you see them as less valuable than others.

Sometimes, a response has nothing to do with work, but they are carrying over the anger or fear of a personal matter and they are unable to separate the emotion of their homelife from their personal life.

Jackie's Story

I once supported a multiunit manager to whom many business partners dreaded speaking. Each conversation with her was arduous. She would become defensive and push back on every issue that was brought to the surface. In her eyes, her team was perfect, and there was nothing they could do wrong. She always had an excuse to justify a questionable leadership decision and didn't seem to care one bit about employee perceptions, filed lawsuits, or employee relations claims.

This multiunit manager's name was Jackie. Jackie was seen among the executive team as ignorant and difficult to work with. Conversations with Jackie were painful and escalated quickly, and it was typically next to impossible to get a word in edgewise.

There was one instance where a particular location became very noisy. Every week, multiple complaints were filed against the leader in this location. Some of the claims were targeting, discrimination, retaliation, and bullying—pretty heavy claims. And frankly, most of the claims revealed some very concerning behavior from the leader of the store. It was my responsibility to inform Jackie of the complaints and the findings of my investigation. I was dreading the conversation, anticipating that she would give a lot of pushback, make excuses, and disregard the facts that I knew created exponential risk to the company.

Despite my anticipation of Jackie's response, I made the call. The conversation was just as brutal as I had anticipated. She even threw in some personal digs that were intended to undermine my position and the quality of my guidance and to disregard my findings altogether. It was one of the most insulting and upsetting conversations I had had in my professional career.

Every conversation before that one had ended up in a match of power tug-of-war, and I wasn't interested in engaging this time around. Even though I was tempted to respond to each one of her insulting and ignorant comments with my own that one-upped her and put her in her place, this time I chose a different course of action.

I sat back and let her go. I didn't respond emotionally. I didn't justify my position. I didn't disprove her reactions. Instead, I just let her talk. And boy, did she talk. She went on a full rant about how incredible her team was and how they would never do anything like what they were being accused of.

At the end of her rant, I simply asked, "Jackie, why do you always feel the need to minimize and discredit the information and guidance I give to you? Is it personal?"

This question caught her off guard. Previously, I had always bit back with a well-thought-out argumentative rebuttal. But not this time. This time, I called the issue out by way of a question. She was defending herself and her team because she felt like both needed defending. But why?

Jackie and I didn't get to the heart of this answer in one conversation. But eventually, the root cause of her defensiveness revealed itself. Jackie had come up in the ranks of a leader who was extremely hard on her. She was challenged far more than she was recognized, and she constantly felt under a microscope where every move she made was scrutinized. The lack of recognition left Jackie feeling like she had no one in her corner. She felt a responsibility to offer up the loyalty and protection to her team that she was not given when she was in their role.

Once I finally understood the root cause of Jackie's defensiveness, I was able to take a more intentional, calculated approach with her. Instead of the usual reporting of findings, I first started by asking her opinion of the person and what the cause of a complaint might be. This approach was more open and looked to understand her thoughts on a scenario before telling her what we were able to find out. That approach softened her defensive nature and made her feel heard and considered before reporting to her what was wrong with her team. Every time I took this approach with Jackie, she was far more receptive to my recommendations. This was because I paid close enough attention to recognize that there was a message of fear and a need to protect beneath her surface message of anger and disrespect.

Desensitize to Advance.

It is only natural to feel a need to defend yourself and your position when an employee is upset. After all, we are human.

But the position of leadership you hold comes with a responsibility to know when and how to remove yourself from your emotions and instead take a position of objectivity and observance. That perspective allows you to gain clarity and become well-informed. With a complete picture of the information, you can react objectively and responsibly, always with the best interest of the business—and your people—in mind.

That countermeasure can be difficult when you feel personally attacked, agitated, and defensive. To regain your perspective in these moments of heightened emotion, to remain grounded, you must avoid meeting other's anger with your anger. A good place to start is to take a deep breath and pause. Calming your thoughts is paramount in gaining separation and objectivity. (You can always revisit Step 1, Slow Down to Gain Perspective, if you need additional help to find objectivity.)

Sometimes, it's even helpful to put more time between the moment and your response. Take a few minutes or even a day or two to respond. A cooldown period can work wonders in helping you to think things through more clearly.

Another way to gain emotional distance from an attack is to remind yourself that all big reactions are in response to some fear, and call those reactions out by name (in your mind, not out loud). What fear could a response be reflecting? Pain, loss, anxiety?

Next, begin to look for the source of what they fear. Try to identify it by asking yourself these questions:

+ What reactions am I observing? Anger? Yelling? Emotional recoil? The silent treatment? Lack of eye contact?
+ What just happened that triggered their response in this moment?
+ Has something recently changed at work that could have triggered their response?
+ How might this trigger affect their current situation? Personally? Financially? How about in terms of career growth? Status?

Asking those questions will bring you out of a state of emotion and into a place of observance and understanding. Here, you can collect the clues that will bring you to identify the concern that they care about so deeply and are reacting to in the moment.

Separating yourself from the emotional element and gaining the objectivity to see through their eyes will bring nothing but success to your business. By recognizing that emotion is a window to identifying what truly matters to a person, you now have that thing in clear sight. If you can successfully identify it, you can now reap the rewards that come along with that knowledge.

The first benefit is that, if you can identify the root cause to their reaction, you make them feel seen. In feeling seen, a person feels acknowledged and understood. By resisting the emotionally defensive response and instead looking to uncover what someone is upset about, you make that person then feel heard, which communicates that what is important to them matters to you, too.

That connection promotes an environment of trust. With trust comes dedication, commitment, and loyalty. When a team expresses those attributes, they will stop at nothing to ensure that your results are as good as they can be. The effort that you put into caring for their fear in the moment becomes reciprocal, resulting in them supporting what matters to you: your business, your customers, your metrics, your success. And it all starts with recognizing the message behind the message.

Key Takeaways:

- When an employee reacts emotionally, good or bad, they are revealing to you what matters to them.
- Outbursts from employees tend to cause defensive responses from managers.
- Outbursts are a huge opportunity to identify what motivates someone.
- To effectively leverage such moments, shelve your natural reaction to get back in control.
- Instead, act like a detective to identify the root cause.

Step 2 on a Page

The second step to building a highly motivated team is to pay attention.

Once you have found higher ground with a better view, you have visibility to all the information you need.

To identify what might be the driving cause of motivation in your people, you need to know what to look for.

You want to find clues to what motivates your people.

First, look for clues in the following places:
- what they are talking about (both to you and to each other).
- what they surround themselves with (pictures, symbols, objects/possessions).
- how they spend their time off or outside of work.
- the general vibe of the room, the conversation, or your interaction with them.

It is important to stay objective when looking for clues. Don't make assumptions that you know what something might mean to someone.

And don't take reactions personally.

If a person has an emotional reaction—excited or angry—to you or to something at work, pay closer attention. Uncover the reason why that person is reacting with emotion. Know that it is because they care about something that is associated with what they are reacting to.

If you find a clue to what they might care about, advance to the next step.

step 3

Ask Calibrated Questions

AS LEADERS, ALL of us are taught that we should get to know our teams by building rapport. On the surface, that advice sounds great, very professional. But what does it really mean? Building rapport is something very specific: developing mutual trust and affinity with someone. Managers sometimes confuse rapport with superficial conversation, believing that small talk will build rapport between you and your people. But that's not the case. To build rapport is to build trust. And to build trust, you must genuinely have interest in what the other person cares about and values. Simply saying that you care isn't enough. You have to show a person that you care enough to learn about and understand what makes them tick.

Because small talk is superficial, it won't accomplish real rapport. It doesn't go far enough beneath the surface to help you understand why they like something, are passionate about a certain hobby, or have specific goals. When you understand the root of a person's motivation, you have accomplished two very important things: First, you understand who they truly are as a person. Second, you now have the knowledge you need to anticipate their needs and strategize about how to integrate their drives into your everyday workflow and projects. To uncover this information requires more specific and deliberate questioning and conversation than small talk can provide. It requires using calibrated questions.

A calibrated question is an intentional inquiry. It has a purpose and is far more powerful than simply asking the first question that pops into your mind. A calibrated question helps you to obtain the base information you are seeking to find—namely, what is *the* thing that motivates this person enough to drive them to take action?

Actually putting a name on it can sometimes be harder than we think. We often assume that others have the same source of motivation that we do. But that's rarely the case. Each person has a different source of motivation with slightly—or vastly—different values, goals, and perceptions than ours. The distinction complicates things a little because, as managers, we tend to tag those who are driven to move up within the company as the most "motivated." But are they? They are certainly the most motivated to take the path that we did. So, we associate motivation with their drive to climb the corporate ladder.

But not every employee is looking to climb the ranks like you might be. Some are perfectly content working in the roles they are currently in. They may want to ride out their careers in the same roles they are in now. They might be working for you as a transitional gig until they graduate from college or land their dream jobs. And while they may not remain employed by you forever, don't you still need them to be motivated at work? Don't you still need them to show up with energy and a good attitude and to put in some unsolicited effort to get the job done while they are on the clock? Of course you do! The more people you have actively working toward your goals, the better your results will be and the easier your job will feel!

The secret to SPARKing motivation in your employees, including the ones who aren't interested in moving up the ranks, is to find *the* thing that motivates them the most and to connect the work to that thing. You can do this using a series of calibrated questions. One question, or even one conversation, won't bring you to the answer, so you will have to make use of calibrated questions frequently when interacting with your team.

Initiating that step can feel overwhelming to managers who haven't done it before. Some might even feel uncomfortable asking so many questions. But the truth is that the process of getting to know who your people really are is usually a welcomed one. Most of our employees are happy to be seen and understood—indeed, most *wish* to be seen and understood—as individuals by their boss. This comment is frequently reported on engagement surveys. If your intentions are genuine and you follow the format of calibrated questions outlined in this step of the SPARK Method, you will quickly find yourself able to hold professionally comfortable conversations with your employees that help you to identify what SPARKs motivation in each of them.

But don't think that this process of asking questions is one that has to be done all in one shot. In fact, the opposite is better. The process is far more effective when it is done over time. The simple act of coming back to an employee with whom you spoke previously and revisiting a topic they brought up at that time sends a very clear message: you cared enough to remember what they were talking about before, and you want to learn even more about them. And, in each subsequent conversation, you will likely find that they feel more and more comfortable telling you about what matters to them, which will lead you to identify their underlying SPARK in no time!

CHAPTER 7

Get to the Heart of Your Team's Motivation by Asking Calibrated Questions

AFTER SLOWING DOWN, gaining perspective, and paying attention, you now have a bunch of clues: pieces of information that you have gathered about a person, situation, or current state of your team. Don't fall into the trap of assuming that once you have identified clues you now know what is going on. That picture is just starting to take shape and isn't complete. What you have are pieces of information, but they may not mean what you think. You might need more information to fill in the blanks so that you can understand the true context.

It is now time to learn more, validate what you have seen, and put the puzzle together. A deeper understanding of the facts takes a little detective work. That detective work is done through asking questions.

The ROI of a Calibrated Question.

Asking relevant and deliberate questions is essential for managers to master because these questions serve to reveal the truth.

They foster understanding. And they generate honest and fluid communication, which, if harnessed correctly, unleashes massive productivity and great success.

> If all you can talk to your team about is the task at hand, you run the risk of making them feel just like a number. The more you can learn about the people on your team, the more they feel seen, heard, and valued. Make an effort to learn a little about them off the field.

Managers have a lot to gain by effectively using calibrated questions. When used consistently and wisely, they are the key to finding the commitment of your team, even when it may have previously seemed impossible. Questions intended to help you understand your employees, their perspective, and the overall state of the team give your people a sense that they matter. And understanding is what leads to collaboration. Think of collaboration as the birthplace of innovation and growth.

When you ask calibrated questions, the path to building rapport lays a foundation of trust between managers and their people. When trust is strong, the dedication of a team to their leader—and a leader's dedication back to the individuals on the team—is what ignites the power of motivation. The most impressive metrics are delivered by a group in a culture of trust, as many studies—not to mention managers themselves—have confirmed.[2] At the opposite end of the spectrum, a recent Gallup poll found that when employees don't trust their leadership, their chances of being engaged at work are only 8%. When they do trust their leadership, their chances of engagement sextuple to 50%![3] That's a pretty solid improvement, and it only takes changing one variable.

Clearly, commitment equals engagement. Sometimes, though, managers confuse commitment and conformity. We often believe that to be good at our jobs, we have to focus on getting employees to just do the work. But when we bypass the individual connection piece of the process, we isolate instead of inspire. When employees simply conform, they produce mediocre results. On the other hand, a manager's connection with each individual member on a team generates that self-perpetuating momentum that we all dream of.

A Step-by-Step Guide to Calibrated Questioning:

There are different kinds of calibrated questions. Each one has its own specific intention and builds upon the previous. Because these questions build on one another, it's important not to skip forward in the sequence. If the purpose of one question hasn't been achieved before you move on to the next, the integrity of the process is compromised. If that happens, you simply have to

---

2   Paul J. Zak, "The Neuroscience of Trust," *Harvard Business Review,* January–February 2017, https://hbr.org/2017/01/the-neuroscience-of-trust.

3   Adam Hickman and Tonya Fredstrom, "How to Build Trust With Remote Employees," Gallup, February 7, 2018, https://www.gallup.com/workplace/236222/build-trust-remote-employees.aspx.

revert to the last question for which the purpose was achieved and start there. If you aren't sure, just start back at the beginning. Even if you have to start all over again you will still get there faster than if you proceed with inaccurate or incomplete information.

Ask Confirming Questions.

A confirming question is one that gauges the accuracy of what you think you know. Here, we look to establish truth and confirm it—that is, to validate or disqualify our observations. That outcome is important because, if our assumptions aren't correct, we can't possibly build a path that leads to success. Here are some examples of confirming questions:

+ If your employee arrives to work in a classic car, ask them if it is their car.
+ If you notice a picture of a child on an employee's desk, ask if that is their child.
+ If they have a visible tattoo, ask what it is or if it is symbolic of something.
+ If they request some time off, ask them if it's for vacation or if they have anything fun planned.

Confirming questions are an important step and should not be skipped. What if the picture of the child on the desk was your employee's nephew, not their son? What if they were borrowing their dad's classic car because their car was in the shop? Each of those instances could lead you to find a way to connect to the employee. But if your assumptions weren't correct because you didn't bother to ask, you would not be any closer to uncovering what might SPARK drive with your people.

All of us are bound to veer off course with some of our conclusions, so now is the time to challenge assumptions and adjust conclusions where necessary. It isn't all bad when we disqualify what we assumed to be true. When what we thought we knew turned out to be wrong, that is actually helpful because we now know that there is more to understand. The truth opens the door to a new opportunity to understand more, in greater depth, and to connect more meaningfully and build stronger bonds.

Asking confirming questions is the first step in the calibrated question series, so use them often. They are especially helpful and a great place to start when you have a new employee or if you are new to a team and they don't know you yet.

Ask a Question Out of Curiosity.

Once you have confirmed what you thought you knew (or now know otherwise) or verified that something might be meaningful to a person, it is time to go deeper. Questions asked out of curiosity are intended to poke around a bit to learn more. Think of it as the exploration phase. Here, you are choosing questions deliberately in order to understand more behind this "thing" that might lead us to a person's SPARK. How meaningful is this thing? If it is meaningful, why? What else lies beneath the surface? The whole process of learning more is to understand what drives an individual.

Leaning into curiosity can help you to uncover the truth. For example, if you thought that someone was calling out of work because they were lazy, questions of curiosity might uncover that they don't feel confident in their job, or the team hasn't been accepting of them, or their home life has demands that they can't ignore. Curiosity helps to unlock the barriers to communication. It breaks down the walls of disconnection and insensitivity. It builds bridges between silos by helping to connect your observations to the individual's perspective.

Questions of curiosity help you to take advantage of an opportunity to learn more about a person or group. What else might be happening either in their lives or with the dynamic of the team that could be relevant to their connection to the work? This is also a chance to simply get to know them as a person: what is important to them, what they value, and what makes them tick.

Here are some examples of questions of curiosity about a habit, hobby, or a passion of theirs that you may have just confirmed:

+ When did you get into _______________?
+ How often do you _______________?
+ How much time do you spend doing _______________?

Questions of curiosity can also build off one another and take a conversation-like flow. This is a wonderful cadence to fall into because the exchange reveals the most organic information about the other person. Here are some examples that might apply to a familial clue.

After confirming that a picture of a football player on a keychain is your employee's son, you could ask:

+ Does he still play?
+ Youth sports these days are a serious commitment. Do you spend a lot of time taking your kids to practice?
+ Do you have to travel a lot for games?
+ What position does he play?
+ Does he like it?

After an employee returns from taking a week off for their son's high school graduation, you might ask:

+ You were off last week for your son's graduation. How was it?
+ You must be so proud! Has he made his decision about a college yet? If yes, ask:
    - Where did he decide to go?
    - What does he want to study?
    - When does he move into the dorms?
    - Have you gone dorm shopping yet?

Staying in the curiosity stage is important until you understand what lies beneath. And of course, it's good to always stay curious as a manager because people and teams are dynamic and always changing. Questions of curiosity are a great way to get to know someone and stay on top of every person on your team, and they are a powerful tool for uncovering what's going wrong if performance starts to wane.

Curiosity also has the power to reveal essential information that you may not be aware of when teams are disengaged or when people are angry. Having this information is paramount to building and sustaining a high-performing team because conflict is inevitable. A true leader can effectively identify the source of conflict and lead a team to the other side of it when they have an understanding of all sides and all angles. The only effective way to do this is to be curious and ask questions.

Here are some examples of things that made me curious as a manager and how curiosity can be applied to situations of underperformance or disengagement:

+ I noticed that when Jenny came in everyone stopped talking. Why? Did something happen? Is there something bothering you? What is it? When did it start?
+ When closing up shop, we have been missing some things before leaving. Why? What is causing the miss? Training? Staffing? Scheduling? Unreliability? Leadership not following up? Where is the disconnect?
+ Staff have been calling out on Sunday. What is it about Sundays? The manager? A rift in the team? Are they uncomfortable with someone?

Curiosity can sometimes lead you to learn information that upsets you. If this happens, know that it is completely normal. I don't share that fact with you to scare you; I share it to prepare you. Every manager finds themselves in this position from time to time. You will not be any different.

What you will need to be prepared for, though, is how to respond. In this situation, it is crucial to revert to the technique you used in Step 1, Slow Down to Gain Perspective. Remember that your reaction will throw up blind spots, limiting your understanding of what is driving any emotional state. Remaining emotionally disconnected is the key to maneuvering through these moments. So, revert to asking yourself: What do you know, and what do you not know? What are you hearing, and what are you not hearing? What are you seeing, and what are you not seeing? Remember that whenever the emotion outweighs the moment, there is more to the story.

Last, remember to ask yourself: What are you feeling, and what are you not feeling? If you are feeling anger, make an intentional decision to acknowledge that an employee's response is due to a threat that they perceive. It is not about you. Staying objective is paramount to staying curious. Your role is to understand the perceived threat and why it's there so that you might consider if you can help alleviate it.

Learn what you can and make note of what you learn. Stay in this phase for a while. You don't have to ask all your curiosity questions at once. In fact, I wouldn't advise it. Too many questions at one time can make it feel like you are interrogating someone.

Instead, spread your questions out over time. Following up with what you talked about previously with someone can be very impactful. How would it make you feel if you had mentioned a concert you were excited to go to over the weekend to your boss, and the first thing your boss did on Monday when crossing your path was to ask about that concert? Wouldn't that make you feel special? Like they cared enough about you to remember your weekend plans? Regular and relevant follow-up will connect your peoples' passion to your leadership and their work.

DISCLAIMER: Using questions of curiosity comes with responsibility, so use good judgment. The intention is to gather more information and to learn more about a person or the state of the team, but there are guardrails. For example, the details of someone's romantic life or the way that someone looks physically are off limits. Avoiding those topics should be common sense, but I'm reiterating for emphasis.

Ask Clarifying Questions.

After you have validated your observations for truth and have worked to learn more about what lies beneath the surface, you might think that you have it all figured out. But your work isn't quite done.

Whatever you now have a deeper and more complete understanding of, you now need clarification on why it matters. What is it about what you know that means something to the person or to the group? Why is it important? Why is it meaningful?

Whether you think you understand somebody's intentions or are confused by a certain set of actions, use a clarifying question to gain a better handle on the situation. For example, have you ever been speaking to a group and noticed that all the people in the group were looking down at their phones?

I remember one instance when I was presenting at a company event and one person was looking at her phone the entire time. I kept talking, sharing valuable insight, but she was still looking at her screen. After the meeting, I called my husband on my ride home and shared how awesome the meeting was and how many great compliments I got on my presentation. Yet there was that one woman who was just scrolling and texting the entire time.

"It was so rude!" I complained.

I got over it fast, of course, and moved on with life.

A couple of months later, I was touring stores, and as I was walking with the district manager, he introduced me to the new GM of the store. It was her, the rude texter! As I extended my hand with a polite smile to introduce myself, she interrupted before I could share my name.

"You are JC! I remember you from the meeting a couple of months ago. I was sitting up front during your talk, and what you said really hit home for me. I was taking notes the entire time and shared what I had learned with my team when I went into work the next day," she said.

I couldn't believe what I was hearing. And I was so embarrassed. I had written this woman off as rude and disengaged, and she was anything but! This kind of misperception happens more often than we realize.

To gauge what you think you know, first ask yourself questions like:

+ What have you learned with questions of curiosity?
+ Why is the meaning behind that "thing" so important?
+ Do you know the cause?
+ Do you think you have uncovered why this thing or circumstance is meaningful?

The answers to those questions are the ones we need to clarify.

Clarifying questions go deeper to make sure your assumptions about why something matters so much to a person are correct. That kind of information is not always freely revealed. With good reason, people tend to keep this information close to them because it is usually pretty personal or significant to them, and therefore guarded.

To get to this raw and meaningful information, you have to earn the right to receive it. That consent requires trust, which can only be granted after you have a complete understanding of the person you are speaking to. If you ask questions with curiosity effectively, you will naturally earn this trust.

Getting to that stage of clarification cannot be rushed. Rushing through the curiosity phase and going straight for the clarifying question will likely not reveal the whole truth. So, before moving into this phase, consider if there might be anything else to know before you ask the clarifying question.

Once you think you have it figured out, it is time to ask the question to validate your hypothesis. How accurate is the root of the connection to this thing you have identified? Some thought-provoking scenarios to illustrate certain aspects that you might look to clarify are:

+ Does the employee who drives around in a classic car have an obsession with old cars, or did the car belong to a parent who passed away when they were young?
+ Does the person who has tons of decorations all over their office love to decorate, or did they grow up poor and deprived, so they fill up their space to avoid feeling deprived anymore?
+ Does an employee take an extra-long trip every three months because they love living a lavish lifestyle, or are they are taking care of a sick parent who lives a couple of states away?

Each one of those bullet points is a real scenario of a person I have worked with in the past.

The car guy drove his father's classic Corvette. His father had passed away when he was young. The car guy couldn't care less about horsepower or the mechanics of a car, and you would never see him at a car show. But he loved that Vette and planned to drive it around forever because it made him feel connected to his father, who he had loved so much.

The person with a decorated office grew up in a third-world country, and filling her office up with things reminded her that she was no longer a prisoner of that world. The decorations reminded her that she was free.

The employee who took extra-long trips every quarter had a sick mother out of state, and he and his siblings rotated traveling to visit her for a couple of weeks every month so that she never felt alone because to them, family was everything.

The circumstance behind why something is so important to someone is the key to implementing the SPARK Method. So, you have to be sure to find it. Here are some examples of how to ask questions to reveal the deeper meaning:

+ Car guy: If you don't love classic cars, don't go to car shows, and couldn't care less about car magazines, why do you love this car so much?
+ Decorator: I am so impressed with how much detail you put into designing your office space. What drives you to put so much thought into it?
+ Traveler: I am happy to grant your time off, but I have always wondered something. It seems like you always take time off at the end of the quarter. Why is that?

Such questions are less about learning about the thing and more about learning about why the thing matters. And that is what a clarifying question should aim to do.

Consensus Questions.

Calibrated questions are impactful in helping you to understand what makes individuals tick, like in the examples above. But sometimes motivation needs to happen as a group, and that is when consensus questions come into play. Intended to calibrate a group's motivation rather than an individual's, consensus questions have a different objective: to align on a specific group goal and collaborate on the group SPARK.

The best use of consensus questions is in a team setting. Applying the series of calibrated questions to a group in an accelerated way can have a huge upside. Either in a formal meeting or in happenstance, consensus questions can expedite aligning a team of people to a goal, project, or task that needs to be executed well. The steps to applying the calibrated questions to a group are the same as for individuals, but when time is limited in a meeting or in a call, the strategy is to progress through the steps more quickly.

If you are holding a meeting, send out the agenda in advance. Many like to prepare for meetings. They feel more confident participating when they have time to gather their thoughts and plan their contribution.

The intention of meetings should always be to define a certain goal and to plan the steps to accomplish that goal. The first step is to share the current state of the business, which is essentially sharing what you have observed. For example, where did the business land in sales, and how did that result correlate to the budgeted plan? Where did earnings before interest, taxes, depreciation, and amortization (EBITDA)[4] come in? What project is coming up next?

The next step is to confirm the goal. Confirming the goal as a group ensures that everyone is on the same page. All should agree on what reaching the end goal will look like for the business and the team. In a group setting, the end goal might be defined with a confirming statement rather than a confirming question, unless you are looking for the group to come to a collaborative goal. So, in a group setting, the shift from question to comment is okay when confirming.

Once a goal is set, you need a plan. But, as we have discussed previously, for a plan to be realistic and effective, you have to have all the facts. This point is where curiosity comes in, and this step cannot be replaced by a comment. You must ask your team what they think. Be curious about what your team anticipates for the path, what that path looks like, how they feel about the path to getting there, what they need, and what they want. Ask them things like:

+ What steps need to be involved?
+ What do you need from each other?
+ Do we have systems we can use to get us there now, or do we need to create new ones?

---

4   EBITDA is a common measure of profitability used in business and profit analysis.

+ What obstacles exist for each member of the team that might hold us back from accomplishing the goal?
+ What needs to be done to remove those obstacles?
+ What information do we need to gather to execute the plan?
+ What skills do we need to hone to get us there?
+ Will this project require sacrifice from anyone on the team? If so, what?
+ If sacrifices exist, can we limit the impact of those sacrifices? Can anyone step in to help the others out?

Uncovering this information with curiosity gives you a complete understanding of the road that lies ahead. With that information, you can craft a well-thought-out plan by involving the perspectives and values of those in the meeting.

Once a plan is crafted, clarifying the benefits of reaching the goal, both to the group and individually, is very important. Benefits can, of course, be business-oriented, but the business outcome should be one that in some way supports what is most important *to the people* on the team.

For example, if you have a huge project with a deadline and the team knocks it out of the park, it may have required sacrificing time with family, at the gym, or doing whatever else might hold value to them. Once the project is done and the goal has been met, you should commit to making the team members whole, providing back to them what they sacrificed for the business by giving them some extra time off or something else that they value.

If someone took the lead on the project and is driven by career growth, the success of the project should be addressed and followed up with a conversation about the direction of their career. What went well? What did they learn? As the manager, what were you impressed by? How can you support them further?

Monetary rewards are common. There is an ease that comes from using money to motivate. And using money can be powerful. But its real power lies in what money fulfills for the recipient. It could just be status. Having more money might make them feel more powerful, better about themselves, more valuable. But the effect truly comes down to self-worth, not money. Money might also enable them to spend more time doing something fun with family or friends. It might fund that trip to Europe that someone has been saving for and is excited to be going on. There is always something that money helps to fulfill. So get clear on what benefit the group most desires by using clarifying questions, especially if you are going to use money as the end reward.

I once worked on a sales team whose leader asked us to share what we might do with a huge payout at the end of the year. Hearing all the incredible plans that people had for a potential monetary payout was inspiring and aligned everyone on the team with an understanding of a value that each had in reaching the goal. It got us all pumped, not only for ourselves, but for each other. We were excited for one another because we knew the impact the money could have on each person on our team. That knowledge and anticipation connected us to a common goal and fostered support and collaboration throughout the project. Asking the group a clarifying question about their hopes and plans for a monetary payout was an impactful way to end the meeting.

Key Takeaways:

- Calibrated questions seek to identify what makes someone tick.
- There are four types of calibrated questions, and each one builds off the rest.
  - Confirming questions validate what you think you know about a clue.
  - Questions of curiosity help you learn more.
  - Clarifying questions help you to validate why something is meaningful.
  - Consensus questions help you align on a group goal and understanding of the group's motives.
- Once you verify that a clue is important, use questions of curiosity to poke around a bit to learn more about what the clue really means and why it matters.
- Once you have learned more, you want to make sure that what you understand to be the root driver of a person's motivation is accurate, so you use a clarifying question.
- Sometimes you need to solicit information from a group to accurately take in objective information. For that purpose, you use consensus questions.

CHAPTER 8

What, Exactly, Are You Looking For?

AS WITH ANYTHING you are trying to find, you have to know what you are looking for. After all, if you don't know what you are looking for, how will you know when you find it? Knowing what you are looking for ensures that every question you ask will take you closer and closer to finding that coveted motivating SPARK to connect to. Without knowing what you are looking for, you will just be spinning your wheels, asking questions, and never knowing when you hit the jackpot.

While each question should bring you closer to uncovering that underlying driving force—that thing that is so important to someone—a problem arises. Since SPARK is highly individualized, how do you know what it is you are looking for?

Here is how to solve that problem.

Although each specific motivator might be unique to each person, there are some general categories that managers should familiarize themselves with in order to help them to home in and find a person's SPARK. I refer to these as the Three Prime Motivators. They are the most fundamental areas of life that will ultimately SPARK enough drive in a person to SPARK action.

These are what we are looking for as the root of a person's motivation. They are:

+ Connection
+ Survival
+ Sense of Self

Joe's Hard-Learned Lesson

Joe was a mid-level manager. One of his best employees, Evan, suddenly submitted his resignation. Joe was extremely caught off guard. Evan had been with the company for over five years and was on the fast track to taking over his own store.

Joe was so thrown off by Evan's unexpected choice to leave that he reached out to me for help. Joe was desperate to know what had gone wrong. So, I reached out to Evan's store to get some background information before reaching out to Evan for an exit interview. I knew that Evan had always been reliable, came in with a great attitude, and did high-quality work. But, after speaking to the team, I found out that Evan had recently started coming in late, was quiet and withdrawn on shift, and was sort of moping around at work. His sense of urgency was gone, and he didn't seem interested anymore.

Evan's boss couldn't identify anything that may have happened in the store that caused this change, but something was clearly different. We now know this shift to be a clue, one that could have been picked up on or explored further with calibrated questions.

With no further information to go off of, I had to reach out to the employee to ask some calibrated questions of my own. When I did, Evan shared with me exactly what went wrong without much digging at all. He shared how much he loved working for the company. He shared how amazing the money was, that the crew was very close, and that they all supported each other. The benefits the company offered were terrific, and he had even signed up for the newly released tuition reimbursement program.

I started to get worried that it may have been something tied to his leadership team. Was it a bad experience with his manager, Joe? After all, as the saying goes, people don't leave companies, they leave managers. But that wasn't it. He liked Joe and felt like Joe believed in him. He knew Joe wanted him to grow in the company.

The more we spoke, the more favorable things he had to say about the company and the team. About 20 minutes into the call, after some digging and probing with questions of curiosity, I finally had to ask.

"Evan, if you love this company so much, why are you leaving?"

That last question hit home.

He finally shared the real reason he was leaving. The company had rolled out a new tuition reimbursement program about a year prior. He had enrolled and was passionate about becoming the first person in his family to graduate from college. The classes he was taking had started off great. But, after the first semester, things had gotten hard. Many days he was working doubles because the store was short-staffed. Most weeks they needed him to work over 40 hours. Unfortunately, the job was causing him to miss classes or left him little time to study. He had to miss classes to cover shifts, and his grades were plummeting.

The very thing that had been funding his dream of graduating from college had been simultaneously blocking him from accomplishing his goal. While the company provided him with the tuition to be able to afford college, the manager's scheduling and staffing conditions had been making his dream impossible. He had started to get frustrated and began to resent his job. His heart just wasn't in it anymore. Getting his degree was more important to him. So, he left the job that he loved so that he could fulfill his dream.

Joe and his leadership team could have discovered the issue and taken action to retain Evan if only they had taken the time to begin to get curious and ask some calibrated questions. Had they been able to identify the issue in time, they could have made some scheduling changes to make sure that Evan was able to dedicate time to school and still work enough hours to maintain the tuition reimbursement benefit. And they could have kept one of their highest-potential employees on the team.

Understand the Three Prime Motivators:

Evan was driven by a desire to get a higher education. But not everyone shares that same passion. Many have no interest in attending college, so they would not be motivated at all by a flexible schedule to accommodate a college class schedule. Instead, they might be driven by career growth, so they might want to work as many hours as possible to show you, their boss, exactly how worthy they are of the next promotion available. But others might not. Instead, they might be driven by a goal of buying a new car, so they might be pushing for a higher paycheck or bonus.

The truth is that there is an endless list of what these important and motivating things are for each individual person. And that realization can feel overwhelming. But it doesn't have to be. The most helpful knowledge for managers is to understand that no matter what might be driving a person's decisions, that something will fall into one of three main categories: connection, survival, or sense of self. Let's dive into each just a bit further.

Connection.

Connection is about the bond that exists between two or more people. When we think of connection, often we first think of family and friends. And those surely are connections that can be very strong. Many will not move far away from home because they are very close to their families and they want to spend as much time as possible with them. For some, the pull to maintain a constant and strong connection to family dictates what type of work they go into or even where they will accept jobs. Another example is the priorities of a working parent. That parent may need to work restricted hours or have a flexible schedule to ensure that they can take care of their children instead of leaving them with a baby-sitter after school, preserving the connection between parent and child.

Another form of connection often overlooked involves like-minded groups, such as clubs, sports teams, religious congrega-tions, or hobbyist groups. Book clubs, CrossFit families, music groups, or even sports teams can be extremely important—even essential—to some people. Such groups allow people to connect to others who share similar beliefs (like religion or political views), have experienced similar life events (like divorce, loss, or recovery from an illness), or share the same passions (like fitness, music, or reading). To those who don't identify with the interest, hobby, or experience of those who are connected to a group, their need might seem frivolous or like more of a nicety than a necessity. But for the person who belongs to a group, their connection to these individuals might be essential.

When we fail to support our people's need to build and main-tain connection with the community that supports them, strain or distress can occur. The feeling of disconnection, anxiety, or disappointment that might be caused by holding someone back from spending adequate time with their chosen tribe can have significant effects on their work. Because they are not feeling ful-filled and are feeling separated from their source of support, they may feel distracted, less motivated, and less engaged. Further, if working for you is the source that is inhibiting a person's ability to connect to those groups that matter to them and support them, the connection they feel to work will dissipate as they seek to regain the connection to the source of their true motivation.

So, if you have employees who are highly driven by connection, it is important to respect and support their time with their respective groups. Doing so will separate you from the other cookie-cutter employers that simply expect employees to sacrifice their entire lives to meet the needs of the business. Yours will become the employer of choice.

There are a variety of different ways an employer might be able to support the need to connect. For example, granting time off, flexible scheduling, remote working, or offering leave of absences for personal reasons would all support maintaining connections in a person's life.

Survival.

Survival is a primal instinct. It has been since the beginning of time. We are preprogrammed to fight to survive. When we are deprived of the bare essentials like food, water, clothing, and shelter, nothing else matters until we get those things. Consistent with theories like Maslow's hierarchy of needs, we cannot advance in our development, nor can we be motivated by anything else, until our need to survive is met.

Nowadays, employers enable the preservation of our lives in a couple of different ways. The first, and the most obvious, is with a paycheck. At the end of the day, money is what keeps a roof over our heads and buys the food, water, and clothing we need. And there are many ways that our employees earn this. Salary or hourly rates are what are most commonly thought of when a manager thinks about a paycheck. But it's not only that. As an employer, you can help to subsidize an employee's ability to live in a variety of different ways.

One of the most common areas in which I see managers lack understanding of their hourly employees is with regard to their schedules. In my opinion, scheduling is the most cumbersome and excruciating task a manager of hourly employees has. No one is ever completely happy with their schedule, you can never grant every request, and people take the schedule you post super personally!

I used to be one of those managers who would get aggravated at how emotionally my employees would respond to their schedules. "It's just business," I would say to myself. "Your availability needs to meet the needs of the business." And while there is truth to that—you have to write a schedule to fit the business budget—I eventually realized why so many would get so upset about their schedules: their schedules had a direct impact on their ability to earn money and pay the bills. They were reacting to the schedule personally because it *was* personal. There is nothing more personal than a person's ability to pay for a roof over their head and food to eat.

However, the buck doesn't stop there. There are other aspects to employment that support a need to survive. For example, making healthcare affordable and accessible to our people is an automatic signal of our support for their health and longevity of life. Many companies also offer discounts for services such as childcare, cell phone plans, and even tech devices. Employers often overlook such discounts as niceties. Indirectly, though, they have a big impact on our employees' ability to survive. For many, that 10% off of daycare expenses could be the difference between paying a heating bill or not. This could be a direct link to helping our employees survive.

Whether we like it or not, the majority of our employees come to us, first and foremost, to make a living and provide for themselves and their families. Everything else is secondary. That need must be met first.

There are, however, a few types of employees who aren't motivated as strongly by survival. For example, minor employees who live at home with their parents don't have to worry as much about keeping a roof over their heads or having food to eat. Their parents probably provide both of those things to them. Another example is a retiree. If a person is retired, they may have a set income that covers the essentials of their survival.

Those two categories of people won't be primarily motivated by survival unless something changes. Instead, they might be motivated by one of the other Prime Motivators, like connection, for example. A retiree might want to keep busy and interact with people, so they might come to work for you for that reason alone. A minor might also be motivated by the social aspects of the job, or earning a paycheck might help them feel independent or let them save for something extravagant that they have been wanting but that their parents refuse to buy. This would cross into the next category of Prime Motivators. Let's explore that.

Sense of Self.

It is no secret that rewards and 'thank yous' are motivating tactics. Employers have used those methods for decades. Praise tactics have yielded so much success that virtually every employer has adopted some form of positive reinforcement into their operating routine. Gift cards, printed certificates, special name tags and pins, or even company-branded swag have proven successful in engaging the workforce.

The reason positive reinforcement jolts motivation into our people is because it makes them feel good about themselves by feeding their self-esteem and making them feel appreciated. It fulfills their sense of self. When I speak of the Self, I am referring to a person's identity; how confident and proud they are of themselves and how they are perceived by others. The Self encompasses how we feel internally about our personal value and worth in our own eyes and in the eyes of others.

The positive reinforcement that so many businesses have adopted has been successful because it fuels esteem and sense of self-worth. It confirms for someone that they have done a good job, which reinforces their perceived ability to do good work. It conveys appreciation for effort, which makes a person feel valued. It confirms that someone is successful, and it encourages people to try more in order to receive the same positive reinforcement.

While attempts to fuel the Self with positive reinforcement can be effective, they just graze the surface of the true power of this motivator. There are deeper and more meaningful aspects of the Self that go untapped or underleveraged by most employers. A big miss!

For example, those who are driven by a sense of self-esteem will look for confirmation of their worth through external sources. Titles, salary bands, and accolades are exceedingly important to such people. They care about their perceived status and how they are viewed in relation to others.

For example, I once worked alongside a woman who wanted the title of her role to be "manager." She wanted the title so badly that she left a great job with huge growth potential for a competitive offer that had less upward mobility but had a title with the word "manager" in it. Her sense of self was tied to status and titles; it was a driving force behind her motivation and career decisions.

While that motivation was true for her, other people on the team, like me, weren't as concerned with titles, but instead were more driven by span of influence. That area of management fulfilled my sense of self because I was able to help and impact more people, which made me feel valued more than a title change would.

Neither is right or wrong here. The important distinction to make is that my coworker and I were driven by different ways to fulfill our senses of self. Although the factors that drove our senses of self were fundamentally different, both were equally powerful in influencing our motivation and our career decisions.

People who are primarily driven by sense of self are also often aware of others' opinions of them. To them, motivation is knowing that they are still doing a good job and are on track to please their audiences. To fulfill that need, these people are constantly looking for us to either provide them feedback that what they are doing is meeting our standards or provide them with clarification to know what more they can do to improve.

In the workplace, the Self also encompasses a general acceptance for who employees are, no matter their race, gender or gender identity, political affiliation, religion, or any form of cultural background. Fueling their SPARK can be accomplished in many ways, depending on which aspect of their identity they fear might not be accepted or embraced. For example, an employee who identifies as nonbinary might feel more anxious at work than an employee who identifies as female or male because they might question the acceptance of their gender identity in outward circumstances. However, they might not feel as uneasy around a group of friends or family that they know accepts and supports their gender identity. Sometimes, we might inadvertently—and completely unintentionally—impact someone's sense of self. For example, if we sent out an email to our nonbinary employee addressed to the wrong name or referred to someone as "he" instead of "she," it could make them feel unseen, like they weren't accepted the way they identify, and this could have a severe and negative impact. In contrast, when the Self is supported in the way that matters to a person, they have a healthier view of themselves.

When we feel whole, seen, and supported as individuals, we

feel more confident and heard. This effect enables us to feel more inclined to jump in on projects, find solutions, and work as a part of the team. When we do not feel supported as unique individuals, we tend to operate further on the outskirts of the team, second-guess our choices and opinions, and not feel confident enough to be solution-minded. Employees whose sense of self is preserved also complain less because their overall outlook as employees and toward the team is generally more positive. Positivity influences our internal voices and reframes our thoughts to be more favorable toward the business and the business goals, thus igniting productivity and a stronger will to put more effort into the quality of work.

The Overlooked Truth of Motives.

The beauty of the Three Prime Motivators is that they apply to everyone. All people are driven to survive, all people need connection and a sense of belonging, and all people need to feel seen and valued. On the surface, that simplicity may seem obvious. The truth, though, is that not all managers effectively understand how to identify and properly leverage each of those motivators.

One big error that we managers tend to make is assuming that people are motivated by the same things that we are, and that assumption simply isn't accurate. Motivation is highly individual and therefore needs to be identified uniquely for each person on your team.

Managers can also fall into the trap of overgeneralizing incentives when trying to meet those motivations. For example, someone who is primarily motivated by connection might be strongly motivated by time with family around the holidays. But someone who has lost most of their family might be more motivated to spend summers traveling with friends. The distinction is important. For some, offering paid time off during the holidays might be ideal. For others, providing time off during the summer when they can spend time traveling and connecting with friends might make them feel more supported.

Another mistake managers often make is thinking that they have identified an employee's Prime Motivator when they haven't. Lori is a great example.

Lori's Story

Lori was an employee of Sally, a manager I had mentored. Sally was aware of the difficult and distant relationship Lori had with her mother because Sally's daughter knew Lori through school. Sally didn't know the details—nor should she have asked, as that would have crossed a professional line—but she was aware of the strained relationship.

Lori was constantly out partying and was always looking to make more and more friends to hang out with. All Lori could talk about was the parties she had been to or the adventures that she and a friend had gone on. With all the talk and missed shifts for parties and events, one might assume that Lori was strongly motivated by connection, and that conclusion might have been a logical one given her lack of connection with her mother. She may have been looking to fill this void of familial connection. Sally asked me how she could connect work to Lori's need to connect socially and still keep professional boundaries.

I challenged Sally to think a little bit deeper about Lori's drive. Was Lori looking for connection with an active social life? Or could she have been looking to find a sense of worthiness by making so many superficial friendships? Sally landed on the latter conclusion, and instead of looking to fulfill a need to connect and have a buoyant social life, she started to look for opportunities to compliment Lori on work well done.

Once Sally started to positively acknowledge when she did something well, all saw a quick change in Lori. Suddenly, she wasn't calling out as much. She was awake and involved with the job. On the surface, it had seemed like connection was Lori's Primary (and sole) Motivator, but Lori's actions were only symptomatic of her true drive: her need to feel worthy and have a sense of self-esteem. Sally's compliments and acknowledgment of a job well done fulfilled that need in Lori.

Guardrails to Finding the True Motivator.

Uncovering the true motivator takes attention and intentional questions. Without intentional questions, Joe was left clueless to the void he was creating between Evan's dream of being the first in his family to earn a college degree and his commitment to working for Joe. And without objectively considering the clues and answers to calibrated questions, Sally would never have realized that Lori's real motivator was her sense of self, not connection.

But a worthwhile distinction to note exists between Evan's situation and Lori's. Evan's situation was personal to him, but it would not necessarily have been offensive or intrusive for Joe to ask questions about Evan's aspirations to go to college. In Lori's situation, on the other hand, Sally asking too many probing questions would have been overstepping in Lori's personal life. So, assuming we didn't know all the information up front, which of course we rarely do, where is the professional and personal line, and how do you know when you are about to cross it?

While there isn't a neatly drawn black-and-white line there, it is best to understand some general guardrails and operate within them. First, understand that your job is to recognize who your employees are as people, not to befriend them or be their therapist. Acknowledging and learning about platonic interests and why someone is so interested in a certain topic is typically fine. But if that topic is not G-rated, or the information they share becomes so detailed that you begin to know who said what and who did what, you are crossing into far more information than any manager needs to (or should) know.

Staying within the guardrails is particularly important because there could be serious legal repercussions if you cross a line. From a business perspective, employees—and especially managers—are highly advised to stay away from conversations that may draw attention to the way someone looks and to never make comments about someone's sexual orientation, religion, race, or skin color. These are protected classes and drawing attention to them poses serious legal risk. There are plenty of questions to ask that steer clear of these subjects, so stick to the guardrails.

As you ask calibrated questions, however, you might unintentionally ask a question that makes someone uncomfortable. In such instances, it is essential to have mastered the material in the fourth step of SPARK: Read the Response Signs.

People give verbal and nonverbal signs that will clue you in to when someone is comfortable sharing meaningful things and when they are not. An employee might show that you have crossed a line by crossing their arms, giving an offended or surprised look, or even giving short, one-word answers to your questions. If they begin to show signs that they are uncomfortable, simply back away. But as long as your intent is to genuinely learn more about a person, just enough to know who they are and what matters to them, and you mind your professional boundaries, chances are that your employees will appreciate your taking the time to know and understand them.

Key Takeaways:

- At the root of every person's motivation is one of the Three Prime Motivators.
  - Connection: Everyone has an innate need for bond, community, and support.

- □ Survival: We are primitively hardwired to find ways to survive, and we will go to great lengths to ensure our survival.
- □ Sense of self: People seek approval, esteem, acceptance, and success.
- These Prime Motivators exist for every human being, no matter their age, cultural background, upbringing, or any other individualizing factor.
- When you identify a person's Prime Motivator, you have found their SPARK and are ready for the next step.

<u>Step 3 on a Page</u>

Once you have identified a clue to the root cause of some-one's motivation, you have to poke around a bit to see how much that thing means to them.

To do this well, you have to use calibrated questions.

A calibrated question is an intentional one with a purpose: to identify the level to which a clue means something to the person and the root driver of motivation to which it might be connected.

First, ask a confirming question to make sure that what you think is a clue is actually something that matters to the person.

Then ask questions with curiosity to understand more about it and what it means to them.

When probing with calibrated questions with a group, use consensus questions.

Once you think you have found something they care about, ask a clarifying question to ensure that you have hit the target.

Each question should be asked to verify that a clue connects to one of the Three Prime Motivators:
- Connection
- Survival
- Sense of Self

Step 4

Read The
Response Signs

NOW THAT WE know what we are look-ing for and the kinds of questions to ask to uncover what SPARKs a person's moti-vation, it's time to talk about the other nuances that go into using calibrated questions so that we can be sure to get to the heart of someone's motivation quickly and accu-rately. Step 4 of the SPARK Method is to Read the Response Signs. Response signs are the hints to what a person is really telling you. They are massively important because, as we have already learned, we must act on accurate information if we are to come to relevant conclusions.

Keep in mind that people often don't disclose all the informa-tion we need all at once, or they just tell us what we want to hear. The trick to sifting past the "just tell us what we want to hear" trap is to make sure we aren't just firing out questions aimlessly to try to get the answer we are after. Instead, managers should intentionally read a full response before determining their best next question.

That step tends to be one that many managers overlook, and not without good reason. As managers, we are taught to commu-nicate and emphasize company expectations, and maybe even the company "why," so that our people understand the purpose behind their work—what it contributes to. That type of commu-nication, called informing, is very specific, but it is not the same as communication to learn.

Informing communication pushes information out. It checks a box confirming that you sent out a message. Like a lecture in a university or sitting on a webinar, information pushing is unidirectional. You sit there while a proctor gives you a download of information, and you simply take it all in. Those modes are great for communicating expectations, but they don't help you learn anything about the person with whom you are interacting.

Simply informing is appropriate at times. But for managers to harness the power of the SPARK Method, communication has to come in the form of conversation. Conversation is different from informing because it actively involves the participation of more than one person. In conversation, each person must listen attentively to the others so that they can exchange information, ideas, and perspectives. Conversation is about talking *with* people instead of *to* them.

It has a tremendous upside. Genuine conversation results in learning something new, either about a person or about the topic at hand. Gaining this information is why conversation is so incredibly essential to the SPARK Method. The whole point of SPARK's first four steps is to discover what your audience values so that you can implement the last step (you will learn it soon), which is where all the magic happens. So, to be successful with the SPARK Method, after Asking a Calibrated Question, you have to Read the Response Signs to understand what your employee is revealing.

Think of response signs like a looking glass into what a person is genuinely thinking and feeling. We all give them repeatedly. All day, even subconsciously, we are constantly emitting signs. You know that term "wipe that look off your face"? Our facial expressions show what we are thinking or feeling, despite the words we choose to share.

The signs can help you to navigate just how many questions to ask and when to back off. Have we landed on a dud of a clue and do we need to start SPARK back at Step 1? Or have we hit the jackpot and found that SPARK in someone? Picking up on the signs your employees send out will save you tremendous time and energy because you avoid wasting precious hours trying to understand something that isn't there or thinking that you need to fix something that isn't broken.

Reading the Response Signs also helps you to pivot and reassess so that you can adapt on the fly. Sometimes, the link between motivation and work was once strong but has seemed to weaken over time. Knowing the signs that hint to you what the other person might be thinking will help you to quickly recalibrate and reinforce that connection.

The technique also will teach you to recognize various actions your employees take to tell you what they aren't saying out loud. To completely and accurately read a message that someone is putting out to you, you must interpret more than just the words they fire back at you. There are many different nonverbal conversational signs for us to read, so many that it can sometimes feel overwhelming. The good news is that you don't need to be an expert on the subject. All the SPARK Method requires in order to identify a motive is a broad enough understanding of the most common and helpful signs. So, let's develop that understanding.

CHAPTER 9

Learning What You Need to Know

HAVE YOU EVER had a conversation with someone where you knew they were just telling you what you want to hear? Have you ever been able to tell that something was up with a person before you even talked to them? Have you ever had a conversation where you thought you understood what someone said but you were completely off base?

If you haven't experienced any of these scenarios, you are among a rare few. Congratulations on your impeccable communication skills—hats off to you! For the rest of us, take heart. Communication confusion is very common, and a lot of factors go into that confusion. For one example, the person talking to you may not be choosing the right words or may be holding back, skewing the message.

What if I told you that even though they may not have been verbally complete in telling you what they were thinking, what they needed, or how things affected them, they still told you in other ways, and you just missed the message? It happens constantly!

Employees tell us exactly what is on their minds and the truth about how they feel all the time. But they rarely use words. Instead, they give other signs that clue us in to what we are trying to figure out. Sometimes, managers are unaware of these signs. Other times, we pick up on some sort of disconnect, but we don't know what it is or how to respond to get clarity.

My Failed Attempt at Undercover Boss.

The first time I realized the true power behind Reading the Response Signs was when I took over a location that was my biggest project to date. It was a broken, run-down restaurant that smelled like a combination of built-up grease and mold. Just how long this location had been neglected was evident from the coagulated dust strings that were hanging down from the ceiling vents, blowing around with the musty air pumping out of them. And it didn't stop with the maintenance of the place. The team was out of control, drinking on site, slurring their words, and barely able to walk in a straight line. The project was overwhelming, and every manager who had attempted to take it on had quit within a month. Now I was tasked with fixing it.

Yoli was a grill cook there, and she had worked there for years. She was a spitfire, and I knew instantly that she was the ringleader. Anything and everything that Yoli directed that team to do, they did.

I first met Yoli on an undercover visit I paid to the store right before taking it over. I pulled into the parking lot in casual street clothes with a friend and my young child. When I pulled in, I saw Yoli, in uniform, at the front door smoking a cigarette—not working, smoking. Out front. Like a greeter.

Yoli pegged me instantly as someone who was not from that town. She was smart and put two and two together quickly. I guess my incognito street clothes didn't do the trick because not only did she realize I was an outsider to the neighborhood, but she also realized I was going to be the new GM and I was paying them a visit to check things out. She was no fool.

True to her personality, Yoli took the opportunity in the parking lot to beeline it over to my car, introduce herself, and, in what seemed like one very long breath, make it very clear to me that she liked how things were there and that she had no interest in changing a thing. According to Yoli, her team knew what they were doing. She noted that a new GM had come and gone every couple of months, so she was sure that they didn't need anyone else coming in there telling them what to do.

I found myself conflicted with two possible reactions. I could take a power stance and flex my title, or I could defuse the dynamic and just listen…

Who's in charge?

When Yoli confronted me in the parking lot, I had a choice to make. Power stance and flex? Or listen and diffuse?

In an attempt to avoid an all-out screaming match and power struggle right there in the parking lot—not to mention making an enemy before I even took over—I chose to respond with, "That's awesome! I am glad to hear that you all work so hard!"

My response must have caught Yoli off guard because she

looked at me like I had two heads. It was clear that she was expecting me to challenge her assertiveness. I think she thought I was speaking sarcastically, so she repeated herself a few times. She used different words each time, but the message stayed the same: You're not going to come into my store and tell us what to do. Our way works for us. You're not welcome.

Each time that Yoli rephrased her insistent message of "we don't want you here," I responded with a similar, complementary response to my first one. After a couple of rounds, I thanked Yoli and came into the restaurant with my family to give it a try.

The meal was awful, and the experience was dismal—probably the worst I had ever had eating anywhere. But I didn't say a word about it. I just took some mental notes.

Over the next few weeks, after formally taking over the store as its GM, I spent a lot of time with Yoli—probably more than she would have liked. In the beginning, I had to spend a lot of time cleaning and organizing in the mornings, and that need got me out of the office and interacting with Yoli. I took the time as an opportunity to slow down on driving the business a bit and to start to interpret the messages that Yoli was putting out.

Even though it was clear that Yoli was calling the shots, she wasn't allowing a total free-for-all. Yoli cared about the store. She would direct the team to prep and clean, and she made sure they were stocked up and prepared for rushes. The only issue was that she didn't direct the team to follow the company standards. She directed to her personal standards.

Many times, after Yoli completed a task and it wasn't done right, I was tempted to step in and just do it myself. That approach would not have been helpful. It would have sent a message that Yoli's effort wasn't good enough and that I didn't think she was capable of getting it right. If you find yourself in a similar spot, instead of fixing it yourself, recognize the effort and then share with the leader or the team what you would like to see instead.

I also noticed that Yoli was also always in a heightened state of defensiveness. From what I could tell, this was with good reason because past managers had clearly beaten her down. They had criticized her every move, telling her over and over again everything she did wrong. And they had ordered her around from their perch. I took a different approach.

I always made it a point never to ask my team to do anything I wouldn't do, so I frequently cleaned with them. That tactic was smart because, while we were cleaning together, Yoli started opening up. She told me stories of how managers would scream and talk down to her. She also told me stories of how managers didn't last in her store because the crew ganged up on them and made them quit.

When I asked Yoli questions about the team, her demeanor was very different. She beamed from eye to eye. It was clear that she loved her team. But, like flipping a switch, as soon as I went back to asking her about previous managers, her entire demeanor changed. It was like you could see her esteem recoil. Her face would turn very stern, and she would begin speaking much faster and much louder. I could tell how belittled she felt by those people, not just from the stories she told, but from the visible physical reaction she had to the topic of previous management. Yoli's physical reaction made one thing clear to me: they had never had a manager who cared about their success or saw them as people, and both factors offended them.

I continued learning from Yoli's stories and asking her questions about working in this location. By the end of the first month, it was quarterly quality inspection time. We needed to pass this inspection. The restaurant was cleaner and was functioning a little better. Still, once I started to suggest the changes that needed to be made in the kitchen to pass this inspection, Yoli immediately met my direction with resistance and pushback...

After weeks of working alongside Yoli and trying to be empathetic to what she had gone through in the store over the last few years, my patience started to run thin. There were times I wanted to bluntly react to her resistance with a short "Listen, can you please just do what I am telling you?" But I held back because I knew that if I took that route, I would immediately be pegged as the same kind of manager as everyone else before me. Instead, I had to slow down, get some perspective, step back, and consider why Yoli was so argumentative and resistant to my direction.

Things aren't always what we think.

It's easy to assume we understand someone's response, and it's easy to jump to conclusions about a response. Everyone does it.

When we have so much going on, we begin to get distracted from the task at hand to just get stuff done. The never-ending to-do list looms over our thoughts. The urgency over a pending matter pulls us away from the message that is being conveyed to us. Or maybe it's just lunch time and we have become distracted by hunger. Unintentionally, that preoccupation causes us to focus on what we are feeling and thinking instead of hearing what our employees are telling us.

Completely and objectively hearing an unfiltered message requires us to actively absorb all of what any employee is telling us. The more we know and understand a person's viewpoint and what matters to them, the better positioned we are to make sound decisions that support and benefit everyone on the team. The more perspectives we understand, the better we can anticipate how they might respond. We can also better consider them while we create new processes so that we can proactively resolve a potential problem before it becomes one.

When we hear a team member's message completely, it shows that what they are saying and feeling matters. When we understand a message completely, we show that we care enough about them to listen. Proactively considering a perspective that we have learned while Reading the Response Signs sends a clear message back that they are important to us and to the team.

The process builds trust—trust that you understand them, trust that you will support them—and then they don't have to worry. When employees have real trust in their leader and their company, they are loyal, devoted, and committed. They are committed to projects, they are committed to financial results, and they are committed to working for you for a very long time.

As you become more and more aware of the truth of what is going on with your employees, they let you in more. They will share details about projects, shifts they worked, customer experiences. That connection gives you a deeper understanding of what is truly going on with your business. It prevents you from missing important information. The more you know, the better positioned you are to excel.

Managers often miss the signs of a team that isn't feeling seen, heard, or connected. If you are seeing any of these signs, you likely have a scenario where there is a lack of trust, and you could benefit from some more intentional, unbiased listening. Some signs include the following:

+ Employees avoid answering questions.
+ Employees avoid seeing or talking to you altogether.
+ Employees avoid eye contact when you are talking to them.
+ Employees are reluctant to share information.

Each of those scenarios indicates a lack of trust. If an employee doesn't trust you, they won't reveal to you what is important to them. So, it is time to activate the listening skills and begin to hear what they are really saying.

What Yoli Taught Me.

So back to the inspection story. While cooking on the line with her one day, I told Yoli that we were in a new quarter, which meant new inspections. True to form, she immediately got aggravated and annoyed. She started talking about how she hated having inspectors poke around in all her stuff; they got in her way and asked her all kinds of annoying questions. I laughed a bit because, frankly, she was right. Yoli went on to tell me how they were like vultures looking for blood, and they didn't stop until they found every little thing wrong. Her voice got louder and louder. At one point, she was yelling about how nitpicky the inspectors were. Her arms were flying, veins were popping out in her neck, and she even started to slam pots and pans around. She was getting very heightened in telling me this story.

After hearing and seeing how upset Yoli got about the inspectors, it was clear what was upsetting her. Yoli was angry that everyone treated her like she didn't know what she was doing. She saw managers and inspectors coming in, flexing their authority, criticizing her every move, and giving feedback with the belief that they thought they were better than her. More powerful. More important.

Understanding what a person truly cares about requires a read of all the messages they convey to you. So, we have to know the signs, and we have to read all signals accurately. To do it all—not to mention well—we have to be tuned in to all the different ways an employee tells us their message.

In Yoli's case, her vein-popping, cookware-slamming response had nothing to do with me. Instead, it had to do with how previous leaders had hurt her pride. A component of her sense of self, pride, was Yoli's Prime Motivator.

All she wanted was for someone to treat her like she was worth a damn, show her how to avoid being "targeted" by inspectors and corporate visitors, and then let her be free, trusted to do good work. But because no one ever took the time to find her passion, she was disciplined instead of taught. The lesson left her with an "us against them" mentality.

I would have failed like every other manager before me if I had attempted to motivate Yoli by teaching her why it was necessary to label containers, why it was essential to clean gaskets, or why it was crucial to filter oil in fryolators. Just like the others before me, I would have made her feel inadequate and become defensive. Defensiveness is always a direct response to a perceived danger or threat. In Yoli's eyes, that approach would have been a threat to her already damaged self-esteem.

Instead, I chose to recognize that there was a reason behind her reaction. If I was going to motivate Yoli, I had to find a way to teach her so that she felt empowered and in control.

I knew that if I could tap into that level of passion and flip it from being defensive to connected to the work, Yoli would be unstoppable. She already had the following of the rest of the team. I just needed her on my side and pushing my message. So, instead of telling Yoli what she must do to pass inspections, I offered her an advance view of the sheet that the inspectors would be using. With it, she would know what to expect before they even arrived.

At first, she was entertained by this offer. She accused me of cheating! But when I explained to her that it wasn't cheating at all and that the goal was for her to know what they expected, she got excited. It was almost like she thought she would be beating the inspectors at their own game.

The thought of knowing the answers before the inspector got there made Yoli feel empowered and in control. She ran with it. She asked me to do mock inspections on her. She even did mock inspections on the rest of the team so that they didn't let the inspectors "win" either. From that point on, we were unstoppable and went from being the worst-performing store in the state to the best. It had nothing to do with holding Yoli accountable and everything to do with recognizing a force within Yoli and lighting up that SPARK.

After figuring out Yoli and countless others, there are a few tactics that I have picked up along the way that have helped me to be effective at identifying what someone is *really* saying. Here they are.

Step back and let them talk.

The first step to Reading the Response Signs well is to simply stop talking. As managers, we often get an urge when talking to another person to jump in and give them advice. That tendency is true for everyone, but it is especially prominent in managers.

Why? Well, because it is our job to solve things. We are expected to put out fires, teach, train, and move right along. So it only feels natural to jump in, tell a person what to do and how to do it the right way, and then move onto the next task.

There are also times when we tend to share similar stories to try to connect. We believe that finding common ground connects us somehow, making us relatable, even likeable. But it doesn't always work that way. In fact, it seldom does.

When we jump into a conversation with a solution to save the day—or with advice or to share a similar story—we shift the conversation from being about the other person and make it about us. The effect is counterproductive. It sends a message back to them that our experience or knowledge is more important than theirs, so we aren't interested in hearing what they have to say.

The point of talking less is to learn about the other person: what they care about, what they think is important. When we resist the urge to jump into the conversation with our piece, when we give a person space to talk, explain themselves fully, and share every thought, we reinforce the integrity and importance of their perspective, their experience, their lesson. And we learn more about them.

So, to begin Reading the Response Signs, step back and just let them talk.

Are you picking up what they are putting down.

Absorbing all the information without filtering out assumptions and bias isn't easy. Truthfully, no matter how skilled we are or become at listening, there will still be times where we misinterpret the message. We are human. It happens.

Any derailment in finding someone's SPARK leads you away from what they are telling you. What can you do? There is a useful tool that you can use to help ensure that you are picking up what they are putting down. The experts call it paraphrasing. My simplified term is this: reword it.

When you reword a message, you identify the main point being communicated to you, put it into your words, and repeat it back. Rewording is the one exception to the rule of talking less and listening more. It is important sometimes to interject with a question to validate that you understand what someone is sharing with you. A rewording is always asked in the form of the question, and the question is posed with an intention of curiosity and understanding. It might look something like this:

"I don't mean to cut you off; I want to hear more. But I also want to make sure that I am understanding so far. What I am hearing is that when the comp structure changed, it made it harder for you to be eligible for a bonus. Is that right?"

This approach starts off by making it clear that you want to hear more about what they are telling you, which reassures them that you are still listening and aren't checking out of the conversation.

Setting the record straight as to the reason you are interrupting them—to make sure you understand—further reinforces that you care about what they are telling you. Finally, summarizing the gist of what they are telling you, in your own words, shows them that you recognize what they are saying and feeling.

Once they have confirmed that you are following their lead, you are perfectly positioned to ask another calibrated question. In the case of the bonus structure example, a helpful calibrated question of curiosity might be "Help me understand how. What part of the new structure makes it harder for you to bonus like you did before?"

The relationship of asking questions and then reading responses is cyclical. One continuously builds off the other. The process ensures that you are absorbing all the information they are giving you.

Listen with Your Eyes.

That first time I met Yoli in the parking lot, I could tell that she was defensive before she even spoke a word. As she walked up to my car, she was on a mission, she walked heavily, her arms swinging intently, making eye contact with me the whole time. When she first saw me get out of my car, she looked at me with a confused look. She even pursed her lips a bit, signaling that she was agitated and defensive.

She also half faced away from me as she spoke. Her feet never pointed straight at me. Her body position indicated to me that she was not interested in me or what I had to say. She came over to state her piece and get out.

When she spoke to me, her voice was intense. Borderline yelling. She was straight and curtly to the point. She made her position known, and she wasn't up for chatting.

I read her message loud and clear before she even spoke a word. She did not want me there and wanted to intimidate me away.

You see, when triggered by an action or a question, we all respond with a range of signals, most of which are not verbal. The signals communicate our feelings and intentions, regardless of the words we speak. Our posture, facial expressions, hand gestures, and body position are all windows into the truth of what we are feeling and thinking. Reading all the signals is how we can bridge the gap to understand what someone cares about. So, it is crucial that we follow the road map of messages that our employees lay out for us. Their behavior will direct us to find that thing that makes them tick.

The more successful managers know how to read their people. Yet, when I first start working with new leaders, many don't initially see the value in finding an employee's motivation. They can be overwhelmed by all the signs they should pay attention to. They feel like it is easier to ask a question, get an answer, and take that response at face value. Any more effort on their part feels like resistance to that pesky need for speed that we all have these days.

Managers who feel that way are a byproduct of not completely understanding their role. Yes, a manager's role is to plan, direct, hold accountable, and drive performance. But you can't do everything by yourself. You need your people. They are the ones doing the work, so you need them to want to do it. Because each person is unique, with different goals, different interests, and in different stages of life, a manager's role includes understanding what makes each of your people tick.

Reading the full range of responses helps to ensure that you are on the right track when you are on the quest to identifying a person's motives.

To read the complete message, you must gather all of the information. Instead of simply listening to what they are saying, study how they are saying it. Consider these signals:

+ Are they choosing optimistic words? If so, the choice might mean they care about the topic and may be excited about what you are telling them.
+ Are their arms folded with a blank look on their face? If so, it signals that they aren't interested, don't care, and are bored. Keep moving.
+ Is their body turned away from you and are they making little eye contact? Again, they are likely uninterested. But they could also be hurt or mad. Ask more questions here to determine which it is. Being hurt or mad indicates that they might care about something!
+ Are they slumped over with their head down, gazing into space? They are probably bored. They don't care—at least not about what you are discussing. Keep looking for that thing that ignites a SPARK.

+ Are they fidgeting or doodling? More than likely, they are disconnected and uninterested. They don't care much about the topic. Move along.
+ Are their feet pointing in your direction and are they making eye contact? *Bingo!* You are on to something. Keep going.
+ Are they closing in on you in an angry haste? Resist the urge to get defensive. Something is there beneath the surface. They wouldn't be this emotionally heightened if they didn't care. Try to deescalate and learn more.

Learning to read these responses gives you clear direction to know if you are onto something that holds meaning to them or if you aren't even in the ballpark. Picking up on these nonverbal cues can be a game changer when getting to know your people. If I hadn't read Yoli's attitude successfully, I would have never been able to identify what she needed from me, and I never would have ignited the spark of motivation that catapulted the team to a new level. I would have written her off as a disgruntled employee who wasn't worth saving, just like everyone else had. But I saw more in her because I knew what to look for and what the signs meant. It paid off big time!

Once I secured her trust and gave her mine, the store that had been deemed the black plague was soon outperforming the top stores in the country. We were up double digits in sales, customer traffic more than doubled, and our metrics were flashing top five in the company consistently. I never could have done it without Yoli.

Key Takeaways:

- Reading the Response Signs is an essential skill to master to ensure you are taking in all of the relevant information.
- Remember that there is always a message behind the message.
- Make sure to give them space to talk, vent, and let it all out so that you can hear the complete message.
- Resist the urge to interrupt and resolve. Just listen.
- Reword their message back to them to make sure you understand what they are saying.
- Listen with your eyes by reading body language and facial expressions.

CHAPTER 10

Expect a Moving Target

MEET STEVE. STEVE was an employee of mine. He was a lively young man who lived life to the fullest. He was known at the clubs by all the regulars, bartenders, and bouncers. His social circle was the center of his universe. It was very important to him. Steve didn't have much family nearby because he had moved out of state for school. He had graduated, but he still wasn't sure what he wanted to do with his life. So, until he figured it out, he worked for me.

Steve loved his social life because it was hard for him to be alone. He was raised in a large family and felt safe in large groups. Since he had moved so far away from his family and couldn't spend time with them regularly, he filled his time with his friends and social group. They didn't replace his family, of course, but they were the next best thing. They were always happy when he showed up, they invited him out constantly, and he loved it. He always felt welcome and was surrounded by people that wanted him around. So, he spent most nights after work at bars and clubs.

Many managers would worry at the reliability of someone with such an active social life. But Steve was a great employee. His social skills paid off big time with customers. Our regulars loved him, so much so that they even brought him holiday presents every year.

We knew that if we scheduled Steve before noon, he may show up half asleep and 45 minutes late. But if we stuck to noon or later, he was punctual, energetic, and highly productive. So we scheduled Steve within those guardrails.

One day, Steve called out of work, which was highly unusual. He never called out. He was that guy who would show up on his deathbed and make you send him home. We were all concerned about him.

At around 11 a.m. the next day, Steve walked into my office. I was completely thrown off. At first, I was happy to see him well and in one piece. But that relief quickly turned to worry. Steve was never this awake and alert this early. What was wrong?

Steve took a seat in my office and spilled the beans. He and his girlfriend were expecting a baby. He was terrified—excited, but terrified. His future father-in-law would not give his approval unless Steve walked away from his active night life and became more responsible.

As we talked, I could tell that Steve wanted to tell me more but felt uncomfortable doing so. I didn't want to pry into anything personal, so I told Steve that I was happy for him, that I knew he would make a great dad, and that if he needed anything, he could let me know.

Over the next couple of weeks, Steve continued to seem off. He kept coming in early for his shifts. He was very focused on his work but wasn't as talkative or lively. I loved the productivity, but it felt wrong. Steve's upbeat and funny personality had completely disappeared, and everyone could tell he wasn't himself. Even the customers started to ask him if he was okay. He would only answer, "Sure, yeah, everything is fine," but we knew that wasn't the case.

After two weeks, I just couldn't take it anymore. I called Steve into my office. He took a seat and looked at me like a deer in headlights.

"Steve," I said matter-of-factly, "what is going on with you? You are not yourself."

"What do you mean?" he said.

"You are showing up early and barely talking to anyone. Not even to the customers," I said. "What's going on?"

Steve went on to explain to me that his future father-in-law had been putting pressure on him to get a "real" job. He wanted him to work a steady schedule so that he could be there for his future family and have a consistent paycheck and health insurance. Steve was torn. He didn't know what to do. He had started applying to other places, but he didn't have the experience they were looking for, and he really didn't want to leave us. He felt like he was between a rock and a hard place. He wanted to do everything right, but he didn't know how. He didn't want to let his family down, didn't want to let us down, and didn't want to disappoint his future father-in-law.

Steve's entire life had been turned upside down, and he felt lost. His priorities had changed.

I reminded Steve of a management development program that we had started about six months before. Suddenly, his face lit up. He sat up straight in the chair and looked me directly in the eyes. I realized that that was what Steve had wanted to talk to me about two weeks before but hadn't had the nerve to bring up. I told him that he would be a great candidate for the job. It would be hard work, and he would have to learn how to manage people who used to be his peers, which isn't easy, but I could see him being a great manager. "Does the job come with benefits?" he asked. I assured him that it did.

MOST MANAGERS BELIEVE THEIR EMPLOYEES KNOW THE BENEFITS THAT A COMPANY HAS TO OFFER AND HOW THEY CAN BE SUPPORTED IN THE WAY THEY WANT TO BE. DON'T MAKE THAT ASSUMPTION. IN FACT, DON'T ASSUME YOU KNOW EITHER. ASK ABOUT DISCOUNTS AND SERVICES AVAILABLE TO YOUR EMPLOYEES AND THEN TELL THEM! THEY LIKELY HAVE NO IDEA WHAT IS AVAILABLE.

Truthfully, I had thought that Steve would be a great manager for years. He knew the job better than anyone, and he had a natural gift of charisma that could light up a room; he drew everyone in, employees and customers. His partying was the only hang-up.

We all could tell there was a change in Steve. His priorities had changed. His goals had changed. He was no longer motivated by big parties and large crowds. He was now determined to give his future family the stability and life they desired. I was just happy that we could be a part of helping him accomplish it.

Steve did a great job through the management development program. He was promoted to manager before his baby was born. He had a steady income that was more than he could have made somewhere else in an entry-level role, he was home for dinner most nights, and his family had health insurance before his baby boy came into the world.

Steve's sudden situation highlights very well something that happens to all of us throughout our entire lives: change. As we go through life, things happen that force us to adapt and grow. And change drastically impacts our priorities, the things we care about. We may suddenly become new parents, like Steve, or we may go through a divorce or big move—all things that would force us to change our priorities. We may accomplish a goal that then resets our sights on a new goal, like graduating from high school and then going on to college. There may even be financial changes that impact our priorities, like a spouse losing their job. The death of a friend or family member, a bad breakup, or a health issue all are situations that can completely uproot and change our motivation.

If motivation changes, there is a good chance that the connection your employees once had to the job may weaken. If you are no longer able to fulfill their new motives, they will disengage from your work and eventually find another employer that can supply what they need. Noticing changes in any employee's behavior is crucial for managers to understand if we want to build motivated, high-performing teams.

If You Don't Know Where to Aim, You Will Miss the Target.

If you are going to successfully connect motivation to work, you have to know what makes a person tick. If you misread that signal, or if that thing has changed, you will miss your target and leave your employee disconnected from how working for you can support their new goals. So, when things change, you have to take notice because you will have to identify the new motivator and connect to that.

Had I not taken the initiative to get to the bottom of the noticeable shift in Steve's demeanor, he may not have had the courage to approach me about moving into management. He could have remained completely unproductive and likely would have left us for the first salaried day job he could land. He would have been unhappy, and I could have lost a great employee simply because the job wasn't aligned with his new priorities. My customers would have been devastated, and, even worse than that outcome, I would have lost out on one of the most effective managers I have ever had on my team. The entire set of falling dominos would have resulted in a big hit to my business.

If the job no longer supports what employees see as important to them, they begin to care less about their work and are more likely to put in minimal effort. They may start to dislike working there. Their lackluster performance can and likely will lead to complaints and negative remarks. And once the seeds of negativity are planted, they spread like wildfire. Other employees who were otherwise content in their roles begin to believe the negative views.

In turn, they also become less effective and more disengaged at work. Productivity starts to decline, and customers don't get the same level of service they had previously. The decline impacts the bottom line. It costs the company money.

Have you ever walked into a store where no one even lifts their heads up to acknowledge you? It's a terrible, uninviting feeling. I seldom go back to stores like those. I would bet that you don't either. Customers can tell when your team isn't happy. That chain of negativity and lost motivation at work not only affects current productivity, but it can work toward building a poor reputation for your brand. Both cause the company significant loss in terms of future success, with the loss of repeat business weighing most heavily on earnings.

Know the Signs.

The idea of losing the momentum of a fully motivated and driven team can be terrifying for a manager. Imagine having worked so hard to build up a team, to get the results that you did, and to build up a reputation. Wouldn't it be devastating to wake up one day and realize that the team vibe had completely deflated, and the energy your team once had was gone?

Sadly, that reality happens often. Without knowing it, managers often miss the warning signs and recognize the disconnection within the team too late, when the effects of the lack of ambition and drive have already done their damage. Luckily, there are signs to look for that will clue you in to a potential disconnection between the work and your employees.

An employee whose drive is actively connected to the work will:

+ be highly productive.
+ actively participate in discussions.
+ have proactive questions.
+ smile while working and when talking to coworkers and customers/clients.
+ be early to meetings.
+ independently hit all deadlines.
+ come prepared in advance of meetings, calls, or projects.
+ rarely miss work.

When these signs start to waver or become inconsistent, it is likely a warning sign of some sort of change. Something is loosening the connection between the work and what matters to them. It might be personal, it might be a life event, it might simply be that they are approaching a new stage in life. But that change indicates that there is very likely some sort of shift in their priorities, and that shift will inevitably impact how their drive is connected to working on your team. So, to get in front of any potential disengaging shifts in motivation, stay in tune with your group often and prepare to respond when you start to notice these things:

+ Their response time lags.
+ Responses become shorter and more direct.
+ They use harsher, more curt language.
+ They begin withdrawing from the team dynamic.
+ They take more frequent and longer breaks.

- There is a rise in absenteeism.
- They become a naysayer and make critical comments.
- The quality of their work declines.
- Their productivity/numbers begin to drop.
- They lose their appetite to be challenged or learn something new.
- They begin to show a lack of initiative.
- There is a change in their normal routine.
- They have become complacent.
- They begin to show a lack of preparation.

For remote workers:

- They become less responsive to emails.
- They start to keep their camera off at virtual meetings.
- They begin to send short, to-the-point emails with a curt undertone.
- They stop bothering to chase down information and responses.
- They start missing deadlines.

If you begin to notice these signs, don't wait to address the situation.

While the details of an employee's personal life aren't any of your business, their contribution to the work is. If that is changing, you have a duty to step in. Most managers step in by doing one of two things: they either try to be a cheerleader to an employee, or they coach by giving reminders about the purpose behind the work, why it needs to be done a certain way. Managers hope that explaining the business impact of an employee's lack of productivity will help them see how their level of contribution will negatively affect the bigger picture.

But what good does that counseling do if the bigger picture, the purpose of the work, doesn't matter to them? If what is going on with them has more impact than your company mission and goals, no amount of coaching or rah-rah moments will bring back that drive. We can't force someone to care about the work that we do, but we can identify what that person cares about and connect the work to that.

We first need to understand what they need now that was different from before. So ask them. Say, "I don't know what it is, but something is off. What's going on?" They might come straight out and tell you. If they don't know what you mean, be honest about what you have observed from the list above. Like in my conversation with Steve, they may minimize it, brush it off. For now, that's okay. Respect that they may not be comfortable telling you right now. You have already taken a big step by simply approaching them and telling them that you can tell something is different. At a minimum, you have brought to their attention that you have noticed the change, and that is enough to start the reconnection.

But don't let too much time pass. If things don't turn around after your initial conversation, you will have to broach the subject again. Only this time, you will have to be more direct in asking what they need. Come out with it and say something like, "I know you said nothing has changed and nothing is wrong, but I am seeing a big difference in you. If it is a personal matter, that is okay, I don't need to know the details, but is there anything I can do?" Offer up some options. For example:

+ Do they need time off?
+ Do they need a modified schedule for the time being?
+ Do they need access to certain resources that you might be able to give them?
+ Is there something going on in the team that you can help with?
+ Has something happened at work that you can help with?

Typically, being specific about the fact that you want to help and giving some examples of how you might be able to assist can get the conversation going. You will be surprised how much you can find out simply by asking.

If you aren't sure if you can help with a particular situation, don't shut them down in the moment. Doing so can deflate them even more. It can make the situation feel hopeless and unsalvage-able, which could lead to them giving up. Instead, tell them you aren't sure what you might be able to do, but you'll commit to thinking it over and getting back to them.

Stay true to your word. Explain the situation to your boss, your mentor, a colleague, someone who may have faced similar scenarios, and seek their advice. There may be more options than you think; you just might not be aware of them. When you do follow up with your employee, make some suggestions and ask them if they have any other ideas. When there is a will, there is a way. Often, simply showing that you care enough to try to support them is enough to reignite the connection between work and motivation. From there, you just have to feed the fire.

Anticipate Life Events.

Sometimes, if we pay close enough attention and stay in tune with what is happening with our employees, we can get a good read on how an employee's priorities might soon change and can start planning ahead.

For example, if someone is graduating from high school, they will likely have a shift in priorities. A high schooler may be focused on their social life, social media, academics, and extracurricular activities. They likely live at home with their parents, so building a future, saving money, earning a steady income, and having health insurance may not be high on their list of priorities. But as a high school graduate, they may be looking to go to college or build a life of their own, and now they might need those things.

Alternatively, you may have an employee who is looking to retire soon. Where they once were ambitious, hungry for career growth, and aggressively going after a bonus, they may now be perfectly happy in the role they are in and want to coast until they reach retirement.

The way you would look to support each through their changing stages in life would be very different. A high school student may value your flexibility with scheduling, whereas a recent graduate might value a higher and more stable pay, a more prestigious title, and benefits. A young, ambitious team member might be motivated by stretch assignments and anything that might groom them for the next level, whereas someone approaching retirement may look to you for a balance of stability in pay with as little responsibility as possible.

Recognizing where each employee is on their life journey can be a tremendous advantage to managers. If we can predict a change in priorities and goals, we can also predict a shift in motivation and can proactively adjust the way we interact with, manage, and utilize each individual on our team. The more effective we can become at maintaining a connection to what our employees value and hope to get from us the most, the stronger their commitment to us and our work will be.

Organizational Change.

Personal change is not the only kind of change that can impact an employee's drive to work. Change also happens within organizations. Internal changes impact employees, too. When we think of organizational change, we think of things like a mass layoff, a new C-suite executive, a new boss, or a complete organizational restructuring. All are events that have a direct impact on your employees.

A mass layoff creates fear among the team, the uneasy feeling of questioning their value, the thought of being replaceable. It can shift workload and responsibilities, so people may be taking on more or less work than they used to. Changes are stressful and make people question their longevity at your company.

When a new executive comes in, it can really rattle the team. With a new leader comes a set of new expectations, new communication preferences, and new personality quirks to sort out. Being under new management is anxiety-provoking. Who wants to have to prove yourself all over again to someone who has no understanding of what you have already done for the company? This is a concern that you will have to help sort out and resolve if you want to maintain an employee's motivational connection to you and your company.

An organizational restructure uproots the team. Roles are redefined, new skill sets are required, and people go from feeling confident as experts to unsure of themselves and vulnerable. The discomfort in this spot is more than some people are willing to take on. They thrive on feeling like the expert and may not be inspired in a role that they haven't mastered. They may not be interested in trying to restart that learning and growing process.

Without doubt, big changes are impactful and can hurt your team's morale and motivation. Yet we tend to underestimate just how consequential the smaller changes can be too.

The First Time I Realized the Impact of Seemingly Small Change.

When I was in restaurant management, the company I once worked for decided to put a limit on how many tables a server could have at one time. The decision was made in response to a steady increase in customer feedback that they were waiting too long for their waiters and waitresses. The new max count was determined to be four tables per server. Previously, servers had typically had between five and six tables in a section. The company's reasoning was that if servers had fewer tables, they could be more present and more attentive for the guests, provide better service, and turn over the tables faster, fitting more guests into a section per night.

Now, if you have ever worked in a restaurant, you know that telling a server that they will have a smaller section size will be received as a personal threat to their livelihood—and with good reason. Servers' income is entirely dependent on tips. To a server, the more tables they have, the more earning potential they have for the shift; the smaller their section, the less money they can potentially make.

From our employer's perspective, smaller sections would not only mean better customer service, but also more repeat customers. In theory, servers could turn tables over faster, thereby serving the same number of customers as they did with sections one or two tables larger. But as soon as we told our servers about the reduced section size, I knew they would take it personally. They would feel like their income was threatened and as if we were setting them up to fail.

Knowing my servers the way I did, no number of attempts to explain the purpose behind smaller section sizes would stick. I knew that their first thought would be that if we didn't care about their ability to make tips and keep roofs over their heads, they wouldn't give a damn about the company purpose or rationale.

Worse, they would surely leave for a diner down the road that would give them as many tables as they wanted—and they would take their regulars with them.

Ultimately, we were able to find ways to better support our servers. We asked them what they would need from us to make sure they didn't lose money.

They were honest about the problems they spotted with our plan. They knew that smaller sections meant more servers on the floor, which meant the food orders would go back to the grill faster. More orders in turn meant that the grill would get more backed up than it already got on a normal night, which would mean longer ticket times in smaller sections, threatening the possibility of turning over the tables faster. Their ultimate concern was that the change meant a guaranteed reduction in what they could earn in a night.

So we supported their need to make tips by putting more people on grill, reevaluating the kitchen effectiveness, and putting effort into lowering ticket times. That accommodation pleased the servers, but they also wanted more training on how to upsell. If they were going to have fewer tables, they needed to balance out the difference in sales by increasing their check averages. So we gave them that, too.

Sometimes, managers ask for input and are met with silence. In this instance, your employees either don't know what to say or they fear a negative response if they share their true feelings. If this happens, find ways to solicit the input anonymously: let them have a meeting where one person takes notes and submits them all to you without identifying who said what; have a drop box for input on a particular topic; create an anonymous survey to solicit their concerns.

The decision to establish a table limit had seemed relatively insignificant on the surface, but it wasn't. Had we overlooked how devastating the change could have been to our servers, the result could have been equally as devastating to the business. Talking to the servers about how the change could affect them before implementing it gave us insight into their perspective and allowed us the ability to prepare and adjust in advance.

Was the change necessary? Was it worth the risk? I'm still not convinced it was. Some locations struggled badly with it, and their teams couldn't adapt. Our neighboring sister restaurants suffered from exactly what our servers predicted: longer ticket times, upset customers, and a loss of their most talented servers, who left for concepts that allowed them to make the money they needed to survive. Why? Because management only explained the business rationale behind the change and simply implemented it without regard for the employees.

Luckily, it didn't hurt our store as badly as it did other restaurants. In fact, our servers made just as much, if not more, money on their shifts. And shifts ran smoother, which made everyone happy. I credit our successful rollout of this change to soliciting the reactions and opinions of our team and taking them into consideration before implementing the change.

All change has an upside and a downside. Find the upside.

Change of any kind can come with risks. But sometimes change is necessary. The demands and expectations of the customer change, and businesses have to adapt to meet those demands to survive. Often, adapting means the business has to adjust how it operates. Sometimes, companies simply need to increase efficiency or find opportunities to maximize profitability. Those things warrant change, too.

Despite its complexities, change can also be a good thing. It can open new opportunities for those on your team who may not have had a chance to move up the ladder previously. Change may also create an opportunity for employees to learn new skills, which means you may need to invest in teaching them new things. Being offered both career opportunities and a way to gain an expanded skill set could make employees feel appreciated because you saw them as worth the investment. Change can also keep things new and exciting, inspiring those who may have felt bored and complacent. You and the company will likely reap the benefit of having more valuable employees in the long run.

Even though most might be excited about a change, and it may benefit the company, it might adversely affect a select few. That potential shouldn't be ignored. For example, moving to a new, bigger location might be a great thing for the team as a whole, but to a single mom, it might mean a further drive, impacting her commute to daycare and blowing up her gas budget when she is already living paycheck to paycheck. What if that mom was your highest producer and most reliable employee? Don't you still need her to see the move as a positive?

Keep in mind that change has the potential to go both ways: it can either build a stronger, more inspired, more cohesive team, or it can create hesitancy, distrust, or fear about job stability. Maneuvering through change can also force an organization to remain nimble. If the pandemic taught us anything about business, the disruption has taught us that the better and more quickly a company can adapt, the more likely they are to thrive.

Since managers themselves might be impacted by any change, they should try to anticipate the many ways that changes can affect a team. The worst case is not considering the impact until after the change has happened and it is too late.

As the manager, keep in mind the most common fears that employees have around change, which are:

+ pay changes
+ changes to total comp earning capacity
+ benefits changes
+ increased time away from family

+ inability to perform new or expanded job duties
+ not being able to grasp a new skill set they have to learn
+ a new boss they don't know
+ new scheduling requirements
+ added workload
+ the unknown

No matter how significant or insignificant we think a change might be, any change we make within our business (operating procedures, scheduling, staffing levels, or organizational structure) affects our people. Change might build a stronger connection to work for some, but it might sever already strong connections for others. In our attempt to embrace the new and to maintain momentum, we have to be mindful not to disregard the connections that already exist. If we don't recognize the impact of change on those who have contributed to our success so far, we risk isolating them and making them feel unappreciated and undervalued. That outcome will inevitably negatively impact the business by weakening the team we have worked so hard to build.

For change to have the most benefit, to add to the strong foundation of engaged and dedicated workers we already have, it is essential to proactively understand their thoughts and anxieties and how they see the change affecting them. Here are some steps for managers to follow to excel in the effort:

+ Remind yourself of each team member's motives and what value your business contributes to their lives. Is it money? Is it having a flexible schedule? Is it being close to their home or access to public transportation? Is it status and growth potential? Is it confidence in their role and job stability?

+ Consider how the change might impact what you have identified above. Will it create a stronger connection between the business and its value to them? Or will it hurt that connection?

+ Solicit the team's feedback before the change happens to flush out any concerns with enough time to address each concern individually.

+ Proactively plan how you might help to maintain a connection to what your team values in support of what matters to them most.

Key Takeaways:

- Life changes, priorities change, and people evolve.
- As such changes occur, their Prime Motivator can also change.
- Maintain perspective to ensure that you still know the SPARK you need to connect to.

Step 4 on a Page

One of the biggest mistakes that I see managers make when asking calibrated questions is to depend on the answers alone.

Many times, people know what you want to hear, or they are trying to create a perception of themselves that they want you to see.

You have to cut through fake noise to accurately identify what makes them tick.

Take verbal clues with a grain of salt. You have to read the nonverbal clues and read between the lines.

Pay attention to an individual's body language and level of intensity (or lack thereof) to gauge just how passionate they are about this thing.

Also recognize that motives will change as their priorities change.

It is not enough to think that once you have found their motivating driver, you have them figured out.

As life evolves, so do their priorities, and so does their Prime Motivator.

Organizational changes can also shift the root of motivation. So, stay in tune with those areas so that you can identify Prime Motivators as they shift.

step 5

Know How to Connect

SINCE ITS INCEPTION in the 1990s, the concept of employee engagement has been a "thing." William Kahn, a distinguished business professor and researcher, published his findings on what drove engagement and disengagement at work. Through his studies, he found something very interesting. He realized that there were three key components to what drove engagement: a sense of meaningfulness, a sense of psychological safety, and a sense of availability for the task.[5]

Kahn's findings were so revolutionary that companies of every type—from industrial to hospitality to finance—have developed a practice of spending tens of thousands of dollars a year on gauging employee engagement and satisfaction in the workplace. And with good reason.

The science is clear: companies with higher employee satisfaction and engagement ratings are more profitable. Specifically, companies that land in the top 25% of highly engaged workforces are 22% more profitable than those whose teams are not as engaged.[6] Imagine how different your life would be as a manager with an additional 22% added to the bottom line of your P&L! It could be career-changing—and life-changing!

---

5   William A. Kahn, "Psychological Conditions of Personal Engagement and Disengagement at Work," *Academy of Management Journal 33*, no. 4 (1990): 692–724, https://www.jstor.org/stable/256287.

6   Susan Sorenson, "How Employee Engagement Drives Growth," Gallup, June 20, 2013, https://www.gallup.com/workplace/236927/employee-engagement-drives-growth.aspx

In 2013, Gallup estimated the lost revenue opportunity caused by low employee engagement to be an astounding \$450–\$550 billion every year in the U.S.[7] When companies learned about the financial possibilities, there was a frenzy to start to win back some of that market share. It was low-hanging fruit, and everyone wanted a grab.

To capitalize on the potential, many companies looked directly to the source to get a read on current engagement. They have asked employees directly how engaged they are at work through long census surveys, quick pulse-check surveys, 360-degree feedback forms, and even outside portals to objectively solicit satisfaction and company ratings.

In some ways, those methodologies have led to success. Companies that promoted an environment where employees felt safe enough to share feedback without repercussion were able to learn a lot about what the business was doing well and what it needed to do better. And when they implemented changes based on the employee feedback, engagement and profitability improved. Some companies benefited from the strategy and got better. And some haven't.

Consider Virgin Atlantic, for example. Sir Richard Branson, the founder of Virgin Atlantic, doubled down on the power behind listening to and respecting his people's voice. If you were to visit the Virgin Atlantic website today, you will see that it oozes their commitment to their people. The message is clear: people are the

---

7   "Report: State of the American Workplace," Gallup, September 22, 2014, https://www.gallup.com/services/176708/state-american-workplace.aspx.

priority. And Branson walks the walk. In his book *The Virgin Way*, Branson speaks about his open and honest communication with his employees—not just those in his exclusive circle, but all of his people. He talks to everyone, from the customer service reps to the pilots, even undercover sometimes, to make sure he gets the unedited truth about what they need and how they are doing. And if something needs to be done differently to support them, he makes it happen.[8]

Many theories have been born out of this craze of focusing on people to capitalize on engagement. One popular theory is that if we share the purpose of someone's work, it will help them to see the value they add to the company. The theory goes that people feel good knowing that they contribute to a higher purpose. Therefore, the assumption is that they will want to work harder to feel good about themselves. At first, this idea found a little traction. It did help to connect a purpose to work. But it's not a perfect formula. There has to be more.

United Airlines learned this lesson the hard way. In 2017, a passenger was dragged off an overbooked plane to make room for four United employees who needed to make a connecting flight. The passenger in question was a doctor who refused to leave his seat because he had patients to see the next day. But the United employees weren't focused on rationalizing the situation or doing the right thing by the customer.

Instead, they were so hyper-focused on the need to follow

---

8   Richard Branson, *The Virgin Way: Everything I Know About Leadership* (London: Ebury Publishing, 2015).

protocol and fulfill the company's operational needs (they were clear on those elements as being the company mission) that they failed to do the right thing by the customer, his patients, and the brand.[9] Instead of selecting a different passenger, they stood their ground and had the passenger violently dragged off the plane. He sustained injuries and the incident was recorded by another passenger and broadcast across the world for everyone to see.

The flight attendants were so aligned with the "why" of United's mission that they did not feel safe enough to use good judgment, step in, and put a stop to the diabolical occurrence that was unfolding in front of their eyes. They stood back and let the scene unfold to make sure the company purpose was met.

Despite apologies and humble acknowledgment of where they had gone wrong with their teams, the company's stock plummeted.

United Airlines is not the only company that has suffered the consequences of this leadership theory falling short. The COVID-19 pandemic of 2020 revealed the reality of what engagement really is as well as where we have missed the mark.

Sure, it feels good to know that our efforts contributed to something bigger, to believe we served a greater purpose. But that sense isn't enough to spark the committed, dedicated, and loyal culture we strive for. The level of motivation it cultivates falls short because it is too much about the company and too little about the employee.

---

9   "United Airlines: Ungrounded," Ethics Unwrapped, accessed November 8, 2022, https://ethicsunwrapped.utexas.edu/video/united-airlines-grounded.

The truth is that there is only one SPARK that exists within each of us that has the power to influence our will every day, to drive self-initiative, to inspire, and to motivate us to outperform our competition. That determination has less to do with the company we work for and more to do with what the company we work for does for us. Now, I am not suggesting that we turn the tables completely and cater to everyone's demands. That action would be ludicrous and put you out of business.

But the scale is currently out of balance. We have focused too much on company purpose and not enough on the employee. We have relied too much on monetary rewards for performance and, therefore, have been outbid by our competitors. As a result, we have lost many key players on our teams. And we have been too quick to dismiss the need to focus on our people as the force that drives the numbers on our profit line.

Some pretty extreme circumstances have put us in that position, but the pandemic especially forced us to reevaluate many things. When we were faced with a real and imminent fear of death, when we were put on a sort of house arrest with social-distancing requirements and not allowed to interact face-to-face with our friends, families, and colleagues, we were forced to reconsider our values. Suddenly, the importance of things like spending time with family and making in-person connections became our priority. Not work, not profit, but personal connection.

Traditionally, Americans tend to make significant sacrifices to grow our careers. We put off starting families until we achieve a certain status or level of financial stability. We take on considerable debt to obtain advanced degrees. We work countless hours to prove our worth to a boss who we hope will promote us one day, instead of spending time with our families, traveling the world, or taking care of our health.

But now, we see things slightly differently. Now we ask ourselves:

+ Is putting up with a jerk of a boss worth the time lost with our families?
+ Is working a restrictive schedule a sacrifice we still want to make when we could walk a mile down the road and get hired on the spot somewhere else with more flexible scheduling?
+ Is the commute and time away from the family still worth it if we have other opportunities to make money closer to home or even working for ourselves?
+ Is the dream salary worth putting our health at risk if we are unnecessarily exposed to potentially hazardous environments?
+ Is this job even worth our time, or can we make money and live the way we want to live a different way?

These are frustrating questions for a manager to admit are crossing their employees' minds. But that's what they're thinking. This is the reality. The longer we fight it, the longer we put off building out incredibly engaged, motivated teams that bring us the level of success we are after.

Some companies have gone to the extreme to address employee needs and satisfaction. For example, to circumvent burnout and support a work/life balance, Shake Shack briefly implemented a four-day workweek for managers.[10] Burger King doubled down on monetary motivation and started paying their employees daily with a "work today, get paid tomorrow" recruiting campaign.[11]

Practices such as offering remote work, giving employees flexible hours to help children remote learn, and providing extensive mental health and wellness benefits that used to be considered a luxury have now become the norm. And many of those concessions are still in place today despite the pandemic's problems beginning to fade. The allowances remain not because they help companies with their missions, but because those companies' people want the freedom. They want it because it helps them to support their three motivational drives: survival, connection, and sense of self.

It can feel overwhelming for us as managers to think that we have to consider one more thing to do: connect to what our employees want. But it really isn't that hard. It just takes some simple tweaks to what you already do now to manage your business. The next few chapters will provide you with all you need to know to successfully connect to the motivation that already exists in your people.

---

10   Sydney Perelmutter, "Dig Restaurant Group is Introducing the Four-Day Workweek to the QSR Industry," Xtalks, February 18, 2022, https://xtalks.com/dig-restaurant-group-is-introducing-the-four-day-workweek-to-the-qsr-industry-3000/.

11   Nancy Luna, "Tech Tracker: Sprinkles, Burger King Add Instant Pay Perk for Employees," August 7, 2019, https://www.nrn.com/technology/tech-tracker-sprinkles-burger-king-add-instant-pay-perk-employees.

CHAPTER 11

Harnessing the Power of Them

I LIKE TO think that out of every catastrophe comes a lesson. If we can learn something from every terrible experience, it gives that horrible moment in our lives meaning and purpose. Many times, the upside to traumatic or challenging times comes when they reveal opportunities for us to later adapt to and learn from. The COVID-19 pandemic, combined with the era in which it occurred, yielded countless lessons, both individual and professional.

On the business side, the pandemic taught us two key lessons.

The first is the importance of organizational agility. The quicker a company can identify a need to change and take the necessary steps to adapt, the better positioned they are to thrive.

The second is the importance of understanding and caring about your people. In my opinion, the pandemic not only revealed but magnified what had been holding companies back from reaping the benefits of truly engaged teams: a true awareness of what their people value and whether they were helping or hindering an ability to attain it.

When the pandemic hit, companies across the globe were faced with an undeniable need to preserve the health of their employees. Health became a primary focus, so much so that companies across the globe went to lengths they never even would have imagined pre-pandemic. Never before would an employer consider taking someone's temperature before they walked in the door. It would have been considered egregiously invasive and arguably illegal. But suddenly it was the norm.

It also brought to the surface how valuable our connection is to our people. Where we once valued connection with customers, we put distance between our employees and customers by moving to remote work or erecting physical barriers of plexiglass dividers between the two. We even concealed emotional communication by purchasing medical masks to hand out to our employees and asking our customers to do the same. We screened our employees' eligibility to enter into our space by asking them to answer a series of questions about their health before reporting to work in person.

In stark contrast, while limiting communication and connection to those we worked with and the customers we served, for the first time in history, companies were forced to allow flexibility to employees in ways that enhanced their connection to personal obligations to family and their own health and well-being.

We gave employees extensive amounts of time off to care for themselves and for family who may have been ill. We started loosening scheduling requirements so that employees could balance working with a new need to homeschool their kids. To support necessary physical distancing, many industries adapted to overseeing and managing from afar. Permission for employees to work remotely challenged businesses to trust their employees' productivity more than they ever had before. Before the pandemic, those accommodations would have been considered astronomical. Now they had become a necessity in order to continue operating the business.

Companies that adapted well to the new norm reaped incredible rewards. Their employees remained loyal, their productivity either maintained or increased, and their reputation became impeccable. Companies that demonstrated that they cared about their employees' basic needs of survival and connection became the employers of choice. Workers who were displaced out of previous roles looked first to employers who demonstrated a genuine understanding and support of their employees' individual needs.

For example, Andrew Kurtz, CEO of technology firm Kopis, shared that his strategy for success was "Focusing on solving problems for our customers and creating a place the best want to work." At the same event, Frank Roberts, sales manager at Atlantic Bay Mortgage Group, said, "With incredible support from the Atlantic Bay corporate office, our South Carolina employees have been afforded opportunities to stay connected, have fun, and prioritize family and wellness." Those opportunities enabled the company to retain their people and to be extremely productive and profitable as a result. And Tara Kennedy, firm administrator from Stokes & Company CPAs, shared that "We try to be flexible and generous with employee needs when it comes to balancing family commitments, professional development courses, etc., as we know those things contribute significantly to overall employee satisfaction."[12]

When companies take action to show their employees that they are seen as people beyond workers, it demonstrates an awareness of their needs, and, when their needs are met with support, employees feel valued and taken care of. The attention fosters a sense of security and trust because the employee believes that their employer keeps their well-being—both physical and emotional—top of mind. That sense of security and trust is the breeding ground for motivation, inspiration, and innovation.

Many times, we intend to follow through on requests made by our team members, but we get busy and we forget. That inattentiveness sends a clear message to that person that other things are more important than they are. Make every attempt to remember, because an unintentional message like this could extinguish motivation instantly.

Naturally, the business benefits from this cultivation of trust. Customers are taken care of by happy and engaged people who give them a better experience with your brand, which in turn produces a loyal customer base and more money spent. The effect accelerates top line sales, making the bottom line easier to

---

12   Donna Isbell Walker, "Top Workplaces CEOs Discuss Their Employee Engagement Strategies," *Greenville Business Magazine*, May 13, 2022, https://www.greenvillebusinessmag.com/2022/05/13/400158/top-workplaces-ceos-discuss-their-employee-engagement-strategies.

manage. Employee effort also increases, which improves the quality of work and produces more of it in less time.

But many managers miss that first step of caring for their people. Instead, they try to take shortcuts to motivation by relying on money. The theory goes that if you offer more money, you will attract better people and keep them longer. Unfortunately, that result is not always the case.

Monetary transactions are a one-time deal.

If you ask any manager why their employees leave for other employment, the majority of the time you will get the same answer: money. And, usually, the employee also gives that reason upon leaving. So it makes sense that managers would assume that the pay scale is not competitive, and they are getting outbid by other employers. In reality, counteroffers are sometimes made, but many times, employees choose to leave anyway.

What is interesting, though, is that in talking to thousands of employees over the years and conducting hundreds of exit interviews of employees who have left for varieties of reasons, my conversations have shed light on one important detail that we tend to overlook. Employees do, commonly, cite money as the reason they are leaving.

However, the pay isn't necessarily the culprit.

The real reason they cite money as their motive for quitting is because there was nothing more than money keeping them there in the first place. There was no deeper connection, no significant tie to you or their work, simply no benefit that working for you gave them over your competitors. So they go elsewhere.

Clearly, the pay structure has to be competitive, and it needs to be appropriate for the workload and the complexity of the position. Ultimately, though, money cannot be the only factor we lean into in order to motivate our people. Why? Two main reasons reveal the dilemma.

First, money is replaceable. There is nothing different about a dollar that funds a paycheck from your business over your competitor's. You can always be outbid. Therefore, if money is your employees' only motivation to work for you, they won't be around for long. To keep them, there has to be more.

The second reason is that when we look to monetary payout to motivate employees, their motivation becomes transactional. If the money is better somewhere else or there isn't a big bonus payout on the table, they won't be driven to put in extra effort. They are only motivated to do more if you pay them to be motivated. And that trap has big drawbacks. You can't continue to raise salaries at whim, and you can't hold a contest for every task that needs to be done.

An extra monetary payout is great when you are close to a goal, when you are looking to inject a quick dose of motivation to push you and your team across the finish line every once and a while. But monetary incentives aren't a source of long-term, committed, and self-propelling motivation, which is what you need if you want to build out that unstoppable, high-performing team. Instead, motivation needs to come from within them.

Desiree's Story

Sometimes, despite all the biggest efforts made by corporations to provide all the bells and whistles of an employee-engagement strategy, we still fall short of connecting to a person's drive to work at their highest level. This happened to Desiree.

Desiree had finally landed her dream job—or so she thought. She had been a stay-at-home mom for most of her adult life and had recently divorced her husband. Her ex was not financially dependable, so she was by herself, raising her kids and providing for them financially for the first time.

The dream job paid a decent salary, enough to keep a roof over their heads, and was in a field that she had been passionate about for years: helping displaced children find their new forever homes.

The hours were perfect. She could work while her kids were in school and be home when they got off the bus. The position also came with an expansive benefit package. She had more paid time off than she had had in years, she was given a very affordable and comprehensive health insurance plan, and the company would even provide 100% tuition reimbursement for a college degree. She had wanted to go back to finish her degree for years but hadn't been able to because she hadn't been able to afford the tuition. Now she could. Her heart was full, and she was beyond excited to start the new gig. She was ready to give it her all.

After about a month of training, she was sent on her first

assignment out in the field, which required her to pick up children from school and transport them to counseling appointments. Desiree would have been more than happy to do this if it weren't for one key factor: none of those children had been screened for COVID, and many of them were showing signs of having it. She had been vaccinated and took all the precautions to protect herself, but she was high risk.

Desiree had a rare and extreme immunodeficiency disorder that guaranteed that if she contracted COVID, even a mild case, she would more than likely die. She was, however, willing to take on the risk if the most basic safety precautions were put in place: temperature checks, wellness screening, and regular testing.

Considering that those precautions were widely accepted mitigation strategies for all companies at that point in the pandemic, Desiree didn't anticipate her request to be a big ask. But she was wrong. The company refused to put those basic measures into place. Instead of discussing the possibility of taking such precautions for her, they instructed her to "open the window" when transporting the kids.

She was distraught at the thought of her boss not caring about her life—literally. "She must have forgotten about my condition. I did graze over it at the interview," Desiree thought. So she reminded her boss that she was high risk. But the reminder didn't make a difference. Desiree was still expected to pick up these kids, who were living in less-than-sanitary conditions in extremely close quarters with no easy access to testing.

Desiree was instantly paralyzed with anger and fear. She couldn't believe that her boss would be so dismissive of a very serious medical condition that Desiree couldn't control. Tears came to her eyes at the thought of getting terminally ill, dying, and not being there for her kids.

The decision was easy. Desiree had to leave her dream job. Not being present for her children was not an option, and this leadership team did not understand that priority. Despite the comprehensive benefits package the company offered, she left that job and found another in a matter of days. It wasn't in her dream field of helping children, and it didn't have tuition reimbursement, but it did guarantee to take her health seriously and ensure a future of memories between her and her kids. So that is where she went, and her new company is lucky to have her.

Avoid Being Your Own Worst Enemy.

In Desiree's case, and in many cases, when we fail to safeguard the thing that matters most to our people, they will leave for another employer that does. It is just that important to them. Their departure will have a financial impact on our business and a negative impact on our team. An open spot on our team means that we need to fill it, so we incur recruiting costs. We also have to spend time interviewing and training. Both factors put more on our plates and on the plates of the rest of the team. Not only do they need to pick up the extra workload while a new employee is trained, but they have to pick up the slack while the position remains open, which adds stress and leads to burnout. All of the extra burden can cause more turnover, which then becomes a cyclical issue that pulls the whole business down. And if the situation is not remedied quickly, you will swiftly find yourself in a downward spiral that will be hard to get out of.

Business also suffers when we rely on external rewards to drive motivation instead of employees' own personal individual objectives and priorities. When we rely on money or other external rewards, the payout isn't intrinsically important. It doesn't have personal significance. It is missing a clear, meaningful connection between their efforts and anything personal like purpose, priorities, goals, or ambitions.

If your boss commends you for a job well done, recognize the people who helped you get there. Introduce your boss to them and share how they helped. Send an email thanking the team and reward their efforts with something they value.

If personal reward isn't there, neither is motivation, so periods of no reward or value to your employees lead to less effort and less productivity. Over time, your employees will get bored with the work because they aren't receiving anything meaningful out of it. And let's be clear, any accolade must be meaningful to *them*, not only to you or your company.

Boredom leads to your having a group of employees who have low energy and who are less focused on and committed to the quality of the work they produce. Instead, they cut corners and get stuck in the "check the box" mindset to simply get through the day. They may even look for ways to escape doing the work altogether and avoid putting in any more than the bare minimum required to keep their job.

Building a highly motivated team doesn't have to be hard. Most of us have all the intention in the world of doing the right things, taking the right steps to genuinely motivate our employees. But many struggle—although usually not from a lack of effort. In fact, they probably put in more effort than they need to. They are just allocating their effort toward unimpactful attempts to motivate. Managers struggle with motivating employees because we have been taught backward.

We often take too much time and energy harping on what employees say they want and too little time focusing on *understanding* those needs and fulfilling them. No matter how hard we try, we cannot force our purpose to have the same level of importance to someone else's personal priorities. Our people will never sacrifice their needs to fulfill ours. It is unrealistic to expect a person to rewrite their goals or put their needs on the back burner so that they more closely align to ours and what we need. And, frankly, in this era they don't have to. There are too many other options.

The Source of Lasting Motivation.

The word "motivation," at its root, is made up of two words: "motive," meaning "a reason to," and the suffix "-ation," meaning "the action or process of doing something." So, to motivate means to give a reason to act. When that reason is external, like money or someone else's goals or mission statement, the reason has limited influence over an individual's decision to act. When that reason isn't there anymore or they lose interest in it, their driving ambition to act goes away.

Think about tracking steps with a Fitbit or Apple Watch. When I am wearing my Apple Watch, I am motivated to move more because it is tracking my steps and gives me credit. But when I am not wearing my watch, I am not as motivated to move and walk because I am not getting credit for it on the watch. Isn't that odd? Moving, getting my steps in, has just as much health benefit when I'm not wearing the watch as it does when I am wearing it. But because my motivation is external—credit on the app—I am not as motivated to walk more because each step isn't logged without the tracker.

For me to truly be motivated to walk more, with or without a device, my motivation has to be tied to a deeper, internally significant meaning. Maybe I associate the movement with weight loss, maybe with heart strength, maybe with being able to chase after my little ones for a longer time and be more active in playing with them. Those reasons have a deeper, more permanent, and more significant meaning to me than what gets logged on an app.

Therefore, if I associate the steps with some core reasons, I will be more motivated to move more often, and the motivation will last for a longer time. It won't matter if I am wearing the watch or not.

That same concept applies to motivating your employees to show up and work with full effort and maximum productivity. The reason behind their motivation has to be more than a one-time monetary payout, or just money in general. The "payout" has to be something that is more significant and specific to their individual priorities in life.

To securely connect to a person's internal motivation—linking their strong, internal drive to the work that they do—there must be a way for the work, the company, or specifically working for you to support or fulfill their drive.

The Solution to the Motivation Dilemma.

In theory, the need to connect work to a person's individual motivation might make sense. But when it comes to the practicality of it, you might feel stuck. How do you do it? Do you have to cater to their every request? Do you have to reorganize your priorities to accommodate their needs?

Absolutely not.

Connecting the business to their needs can be done very simply, and it doesn't require much effort on your part at all. It is a process that can be applied to most of the things that you already do every day, but with a minor tweak.

The concept is simple. The secret to connecting work to what a person already values and needs lies in two actions:

1. **Help them to preserve the thing(s) they already value.** People take action to avoid losing anything that means something to them—time with their family and loved ones, their health and survival, their esteem and self-worth, or their status. These priorities define who they are as individuals, have some sort of history or personal meaning, hold some sort of value to them, and protect their well-being. So, employees will frequently put in more effort for an employer who helps to preserve these priorities through things like benefit packages, earning capacity, flexible schedules, remote working, and basic respect.

2. **Give them tools to fulfill what they are lacking but want.** People also take action when work helps them to accomplish whatever is important to them. It might be a career-oriented goal, where a person will work harder, put in more hours, and be more proactively productive when they can see a benefit to their career such as a promotion. But the objective could also be personal. They might want to earn a secondary degree, so they may put a sustained effort into working for a company that helps them to pay for tuition through reimbursement. Another person may value spending time with their young children, so they may feel an extra commitment and loyalty to a company that ensures that they never miss a birthday party or enables them to be home at night to help with homework and be

present for family dinners. Others may feel dedicated to an employer that provides them with discounts on expenses like childcare or cell phone plans because those benefits help to stretch a monthly budget more comfortably.

Some of those things you may be able to do; some you may not. But it is worth an audit of what you can and cannot swing for your people to show them just how much their well-being matters to you and the brand. So, before you scratch anything off of the list, consider what they might need, understand their priorities, and take an honest inventory of the leverage you already have.

The Prework to Making the Connection.

Many managers overthink the difficulty of making the connection. But the truth is that you already have most of what your employees want or need. You just may not see the connection yet. And often, neither do they. The simple lack of awareness around how they might be able to leverage the business to protect what they value the most, or to attain what they are most driven to achieve, is the missing link to igniting that spark of motivation.

In more rare instances, some employees do see the connection. These are the employees we peg as "high potential." They are the ones who make you say, "Finally, a good one!" They are the ones you tag as future leaders. They are the ones who seek out answers to questions about the work, put in more effort, and are highly productive. But why is that? What is it that makes them so much more motivated than the rest?

The truth is that they are working hard and seem to be self-driven because they see the connection between their goals and the tools or stepping stones the company provides to accomplish those goals. Those who are already obviously motivated might have their sights set on moving up in the company, or maybe their goal is to afford the new car they want to buy, or it could be attaining a title that would make their parents proud. Employees like them are the easy ones for us to motivate because, frankly, they are already motivated. All you have to do is give them some stretch assignments or dangle a carrot of a promotion in front of them to push them a little more. It is clear to them how working for you can benefit them, so they put in the effort.

What about those who don't see the clear connection between working for you and accomplishing their goals or guarding what they want to protect? Don't you need them to put in the effort, too? Of course you do. They are the low-hanging fruit, the ones who hold you back from creating that dream team you want to create. But keep in mind that the phrase "low-hanging fruit" means that they're easy to reach. So, to motivate them in the same way that you motivate the already self-motivated, you simply have to apply the same formula: show them how your work can help them accomplish their own personal goals. But to help them see the link, you first have to see it, too.

A Checklist for Managers to Prepare to Connect:

Fueling any employee's specific drive requires managers to periodically shift into a humble mindset, less focused on our point of view and more focused on theirs. After all, to give people what they want, you have to see things their way. Through understanding their perspectives and considering their ambitions, you gain empathetic accuracy. That true and precise information helps you to identify exactly what you might be able to offer to link their drive to your work. Consider which is their strongest of the three motivational drivers (connection, survival, or sense of self) and what your employees might be asking themselves while at work or thinking about, such as:

+ What are my long-term goals?
+ How can I move up in the company?
+ How can I make a career for myself here?
+ How can I develop into a leader?
+ How can I make more money?
+ How can I work to pay my bills and still be there for my family?
+ How can I contribute to something meaningful?
+ How can I be a part of the team?
+ How can I add value?
+ How can I manage this workload and still have time for myself?
+ How can I make the money I need to cover expenses and still have time for schoolwork?

+ How can I work and participate in my group or club?
+ How can I get better benefits for myself and my family?
+ How can I keep my job and still travel the world?
+ What does it take to just be appreciated around here?

After you have considered your employees' point of view and what they might want from you, it is time to consider what you might already have to meet that need. Start by familiarizing yourself with the company's perks and options.

Believe it or not—and I am sad to say—most of the time, managers assume they know all that the company offers, but they don't. That's even true for many mid-level managers or even upper management. Not knowing about all the perks doesn't mean they aren't there. So ask!

Think about your employees' everyday expenses. Find out if cell phone discounts or other allowances are offered through employee-benefit programs. Often, those programs go under-promoted to those with boots on the ground. Sometimes even bigger benefits are available, like daycare discounts or tuition reimbursement.

Consider also how you are currently operating and what leeway you might reasonably be able to offer. Make a list by starting with these thoughts:

+ What benefits does the company offer that might fulfill what they want?
+ If certain benefits are only available to certain positional

levels, what does this person need to do to get to that position?

+ What exists currently in how we operate that can support what they need? (Think about the different categories: connection, survival, and sense of self.)
+ What exists currently that might feel like a threat to maintaining or protecting what holds value to them?
+ What changes are coming that might support what you know motivates them?
+ What changes are coming that might adversely take away from their SPARK?
+ What reasonable things can you offer to this employee that would support what matters most to them? (Think discounts, benefits, time off, flexible schedules, extra projects, recognition.)
+ What obstacles exist that you can remove to help them fulfill what drives them?

Spend some time with those questions and analyze your business through a new lens: a vessel of support. Having an extensive list of existing allowances or other options that can easily be harvested will serve your new mission of linking employees' motivation to the job. Specifically, consider the person whose motivation is disconnected, and, after pinpointing the source of their drive, refer back to this list for ideas for how to reconnect.

Keep the list handy and refresh it from time to time. The more often you review it and the more often you successfully connect to individual motives, the more ideas will begin to pop. The more extensive and creative the list, the more options you have to easily and effortlessly feed the fire of motivation for each person on your team. Once you have flushed out what is important to them and considered how you might be able to support their Prime Motivator, it is time to make the connection.

Key Takeaways:

- Showing employees that their work contributes to a bigger purpose is only half the battle, so it falls short of creating motivated teams.
- We have focused too much on teaching them how to fulfill our purpose and have passed over how we can fulfill theirs.
- For an employee to fully devote the time they spend working for you to your purpose, you have to show them that you care about theirs.
- Money is an important factor, but depending solely on money to instill motivation makes the relationship transactional and easily replaced.
- To ignite long-term, loyal, dedicated motivation, we have to help employees to fulfill what is important to them by doing one or both of the following:
  - Help them to preserve whatever goals they already have and value.
  - Give them the tools to gain what they are lacking but want.

CHAPTER 12

Ignite Motivation Through Connection

AT THIS STAGE in the game, you have done the "hard" (but enlightening) work of getting to know your people and understanding what makes them tick. You have also put some thought to what you might already be able to leverage to support that SPARK in your people. Now it is time for you to align the two, ignite the flame of motivation, and reap the rewards. It is time to connect what they value and are motivated to work for to the unique opportunity of working for you.

Why is working for you such a unique opportunity? Because now each person working on your team will be working for a leader who knows their aspirations and their motives, understands their drive, and can help them to fulfill those areas of their lives. You will be the leader who promotes their priorities on their behalf, which makes you and your company a rare find.

Once your employees realize your commitment to them, the trust that they have in you to protect their best interests combined with the support they feel will manifest in reciprocity of dedication, productivity, and loyalty. That connection to their aspirations—personal or professional—is the key to lighting up their SPARK. They will suddenly show up with the will to work, and they will have no reason to look elsewhere because what you will now be able provide to them is not easily replaceable.

Ultimately, there are two main ways in which you can connect to what it is that matters most to an employee. The first is through the work itself, and the second is through your actions and reactions. Both have the potential to light the fire of motivation. How and when you use each approach will depend on your employee, which of the three motivational factors resonates the strongest for them, and what you currently have to offer as support.

Connect the Dots.

You already know how what you are about to offer to your employees might help them. However, while you might see the connection between working for you and how that can impact what matters to them, they likely do not. The manager who struggles with lighting up motivation in their employees misses that very crucial point. Too often, managers offer a stretch assignment or grant an extra day off without connecting it to how it benefits the employee.

For example, if Manager Jerry told Employee Alex that he was going to take the lead on a department-wide training program by saying, "Alex, listen, I know you are an expert at this topic and can train it well…" then that might make Alex feel good about himself. But if career growth was more important to Alex than compliments, it might be more impactful to say something like this: "Alex, there is no question that you are an expert at this subject. But I also know that you have high aspirations to lead a larger team. For that next step in your career, speaking and presenting to large groups of people will serve you well. So I want you to take this assignment as an opportunity to start developing a skill that will help prepare you for the next level." Although the first approach was nice, it didn't drive home how this assignment connected to Alex's true drive: a promotion. The second approach did, which would make it far more motivating than the first.

The Strategic Use of Recognition.

Recognition can be very powerful when used correctly. It is a known fact, one that has been studied for decades, that when employees feel recognized, engagement, retention, and overall productivity increase. Tremendous positive momentum can be harnessed through the experience of accomplishing a goal and being recognized for it. It feels good to be acknowledged for our hard work, and it is only natural to continue to want to work hard to feel those same positive feelings of pride, worthiness, and accomplishment. That outcome is so well-known that the use of recognition is woven into most leadership-development work-shops and tutorials.

Surprisingly, despite how widely recognized the power of rec-ognition is, most managers fall short in understanding how to fully leverage recognition, and they leave considerable positive momentum on the table. They tend to wait to recognize staff until a goal has been accomplished, when the hard work is done and a project is over. If the goal isn't accomplished, they feel as though there is nothing to recognize, so they don't.

Whether a goal was accomplished or not, wasn't there some effort put into trying? Did anyone put a lot of thought, time, or effort into the project or assignment that fell short? In most cases, the answer is probably yes. If so, isn't that worth recognizing?

To truly leverage the power of recognition, it can't be reserved only for those times of success. If things improved, moved in a positive direction, and you gained ground, you are significantly better off than you were before, and it didn't come without the effort, energy, and time of your team. Without recognizing the effort that went into improvement, you make a very clear statement: their effort wasn't good enough and, therefore, they aren't good enough. Who wants to continue to work for someone who doesn't see or respect how hard they tried?

Many managers live in the "the paycheck is their reward" mentality. But for employees these days, that reality is fading away. One of your competitors can replace your paycheck, and there are many options to earn supplemental income elsewhere. A job well done needs more than just a paycheck as a reward if you want a motivated team.

If there truly is power in positive momentum, even if you didn't hit a goal this time around, isn't there ground still to be conquered in the future? And if that is the case, doesn't it make sense to celebrate how far you have come and to continue that momentum into accomplishing the next goal? To truly leverage the power of recognition, recognize the effort if the effort is there, regardless of the result. It will catapult you into a winning bracket before you know it.

Another way to leverage the power of recognition is to not wait until the end of the project. Set up preplanned checkpoints throughout the project, especially if it is a big one, to not only calibrate on progress, but to celebrate the effort that your people have put in so far. That simple act will inject bouts of recognition that will ignite renewed energy and motivation in the work, pushing you that much closer to your goal.

What's the reward worth?

I once supported a manager, we will call him Ryan, who had recently been promoted to a multiunit management position. Ryan loved contests. He was extremely competitive. He thrived on having the top results, flashing the best numbers, and keeping his name at the top of all favorable lists. To support the need to keep his name at the top, Ryan constantly had some sort of contest going. He posted daily updates, he called out top performers to leverage the wave of positive feedback, and he consistently reminded them of a gift card that was waiting for them if they hit the goal. Contests were so frequent in his market that he carried around a stack of gift cards ranging anywhere from $10 to $50.

Now, one might imagine that, with a constant financial incentive going, Ryan was constantly flashing incredible numbers. But he didn't. He quickly realized that his results went up and down, and the same five or so people were the ones winning the gift cards. It was rare that any of his other 150 employees put in much effort to win the contests. It wasn't a training gap. They all had the necessary skills to deliver. They just didn't put in the effort. The situation was extremely frustrating and confusing to Ryan.

What Ryan didn't realize is that he was only getting participation from certain people because those were the people who were motivated by extra spending money. The people who weren't putting in the effort didn't see the benefit of the extra effort to get an extra $10 or $20 a month. So, one day, he changed up the reward. Instead of offering money, he offered up two extra paid days off that month, and the winning employee could pick the days they wanted. Suddenly, employees who hadn't put any effort into winning the contest before stepped up. They blew the financially motivated out of the water. These employees were the ones who valued their personal time and time with their loved ones.

The difference was an eye-opening moment for Ryan. Not everyone is motivated by the same things. If the goal is to build a motivated team of people that stretches beyond just a couple of top performers, the reward offered has to matter to all types of motives.

From that point on, Ryan began to get more creative with the rewards that he offered to those who put in the effort that kept his name at the top of his pack. In addition to gift cards and paid time off, there were trophies to motivate those who loved displaying accomplishments, handwritten thank you cards for those motivated by esteem and feeling individually seen, lunches with him and his boss for those who were motivated by career growth, and complimentary tickets to family events like amusement parks and concerts for those who value connection with family and friends and love these types of events. Because Ryan began to tap into the root drivers of each individual's priorities, he leveraged the motivation of more than just a select few. It paid off.

Implement their ideas.

As a leader, it can feel like your job is only to make the decisions. That is true. Ultimately, the final call is yours. But having the power to make the final call doesn't mean that you are always going to have all of the answers or have the best ideas. The longer you spend in management, the more removed you become from the day-to-day impact and struggles in a position or a task. A previous supervisor of mine, we will call her Angie, found that out the hard way.

Angie had been in a multiunit role for about 10 years, and a lot had changed in the company during that timeframe. Many tasks that used to be done by hand were now automated, processes had evolved, and laws had become more stringent. While she was involved with the new processes as they were rolled out to the company, she had never managed a business with them in place. She believed that she understood the way to lead with those new processes, but she didn't fully.

After a few company reorganizations, Angie decided to step back into a single unit leadership role. She assumed that it would be like riding a bike. But it wasn't. All of the new processes and systems that were supposed to make things more efficient often created more work. There were system errors that caused more bottlenecks than they helped alleviate. Platforms didn't communicate with one another, so sometimes she found herself doing twice the work. And the labor laws were so much more restrictive now than when she ran stores that she found herself in the middle of a huge learning curve in running day-to-day shifts. The role wasn't as easy as she had remembered, and she instantly had a newfound appreciation for what her team had been going through.

For years, Angie had been coaching her employees with advice that was out of touch. She hadn't realized how time-consuming some of these processes were and how much stress was involved. She should have used a different approach.

Instead of assuming she knew their role, Angie should have asked her employees for ideas of how to be more efficient and more productive. She should have sought out their solutions because, ultimately, they, not her, were the experts on the subject. Actually, the imbalance became painstakingly clear to her within her first month back in a store.

Asking your team for their input in how to accomplish a goal or approach a project will ensure the point of this book: their ideas are more likely to fulfill their motives and alleviate the pain points than your solutions or direction. And because they are providing their personal solutions, they will also be motivated to make their ideas a success. They will put in full effort to ensure success of a project or hit a goal if they were the ones to develop the plan.

Letting them take the lead will also create more of a team

commitment because the rest of the team will likely buy in to a plan created by one of their own—someone who understands their pain and their day-to-day frustrations.

Moreover, implementing their ideas will light up motivation for those who love to be in the spotlight and get the credit. The opportunity will also serve well as a motivator to someone who wants to grow in their role and move up within an organization. Getting your employees involved also serves equally well, if not better, for those who have frustrations with a company or process for a very simple reason: implementing their ideas allows a person the freedom to find a solution to their gripes and to alleviate their frustrations. Your employees might have ideas to streamline a process, which will free up more time for other things like time off with family (important to those who value connection) or to make improvements to other projects that help them to drive profitability, which will get them closer to a bonus (motivators for those either driven by survival or prestige). When you implement their ideas, they get to be the hero in solving their problem—a problem that others probably share.

Loosening the reins doesn't have to be on big, over-the-top projects. For example, maybe the need is as simple as how to arrange a service aisle so that the flow makes more sense, or how often to have meetings so that the team is still on the same page but you don't eat up precious calendar time that they could use to be productive in other things. No matter how big or small, asking for and implementing their ideas will allow you an opportunity to meaningfully connect to the aspects that matter to the person on your team, which will help to drive motivation.

See their mistakes as learnings, not failures.

After decades of speaking to disgruntled employees and conducting exit interviews, what has become increasingly apparent to me is how important this point is: if a person does not feel safe enough to make a mistake, they will never feel safe enough to put in their full effort. Instead of going in full force with a dedicated and inspired mindset, they will tread slowly and cautiously. When we fear getting in trouble or being reprimanded for making an error, we are more afraid than we are driven, so we hold back.

It is easy to get focused just on your A team, the high performers. And they certainly deserve the praise and recognition that you give to them. But make sure to find time to recognize your B and C performers too. No team is made up of all A performers, and you still need those B's and C's to show up motivated. So balance your attention scales and carve out time to recognize everyone on your team.

If the goal is to build a high-performing team, we must anticipate that there will be mistakes and failures. That understanding isn't a free pass for costly errors, but it is an important mindset shift. Seeing a missed goal only as a failure instills feelings of low self-worth and wasted effort. Focusing on the failure creates demotivating mindsets. When we can identify a lesson about what not to do next time, we are better off than we were when we started. As a leader, reminding your employees of what they did accomplish—and what they learned—is crucial.

If they put in extra time and effort, sacrificed time with their family and friends, or even lost sleep to try to help you and the company accomplish something, but they fell short, they will feel deflated and defeated. They will question their worth and may not be motivated to try again the next time. It is up to you to identify what you gained from a project in order to highlight the benefit from their sacrifice. Consider the following:

+ Did the team learn any new skills?
+ Were any hurdles or pain points identified that you didn't know existed that you can now address?
+ Did you find new ways to communicate and strategize?
+ Did you make any gains in business, even if you didn't hit a goal?
+ Did you identify future leaders?
+ Did you learn anything new about your team or your people?
+ Did you learn what not to do so that you can teach others what to avoid or be aware of to ensure success in the future?

Every failure has learning associated with it. If you find your team or a team member falling short, find the upside and share that with them. It will give purpose to what might feel like lost effort to those who tried hard to reach a goal—perhaps one that you helped to associate with something specifically important to them. Make sure they understand how much more they walked away with despite the missed goal, and how they are now better positioned for success in the future.

Deliver feedback with grace.

Any candid conversation, especially one that highlights someone's shortcomings or the dreadful conversation intended to alert them to something they're doing wrong, has a very specific and intentional purpose. Its purpose is *not* to formalize documents as a means to be able to fire someone later. At least, it shouldn't be. That approach to a candid feedback conversation is the single most ineffective way to motivate someone into trying harder and improving.

On the contrary, the purpose of a candid performance conversation should be to promote someone's growth. The goal should be to correct the shortcoming so that they can not only keep a spot on your team, but also become a more valuable member. An employee should not walk away from a performance conversation feeling beat up and bad about themselves. Instead, they should feel like they have the support they need to do better next time.

 Delivering a performance improvement plan or written warning can be very uncomfortable. The most demotivating and counterproductive approach that a manager can take is to sit the person down, read a document, and ask for a signature. Instead, sit them down and honestly share your concerns. Discuss their perspective and offer up a plan to help them improve. If there is a warning involved, make sure they know that it is to document that a conversation happened but that you hope to sit down to talk to them next time about how much they have improved. Don't break out the document to sign until the conversation has ended and a plan is in place.

Before meeting with an employee to discuss performance, a manager should first prepare their own personal mindset. The simple shift from approaching a performance conversation with an intent to help versus an intent to reprimand will instantly change your tone, expressions, and approach to a more positive and supportive one.

It is also important to approach the conversation as just that—a conversation. A conversation is not one-sided. When one person talks directly to another without any exchange of thoughts or ideas, it is not a conversation, it is a lecture. In true conversation, we share our position while also learning the other's point of view, and we gain an understanding of any underlying issues. Maybe an underperformer has not received the proper training. Maybe there wasn't clear direction. Maybe looming staffing concerns are impacting their ability to properly do their job. Does their under-performance have anything to do with work or the work environment, or do they just want something different from what this job currently has to offer? Perhaps they are struggling with something in their personal life.

No matter the root cause, it is important to understand what has caused a performance deficit because once you understand, you can offer help to alleviate the hurdles. You can offer more training. You can discuss other career options and how to better prepare them to reach those goals. You can offer up some time off so that they can take care of their personal life and then return to work refreshed and refocused.

Many managers shy away from that approach because they fear that hearing an excuse is acceptance of underperformance. But nothing could be further from the truth. Hearing an employee out about what might be holding them back gives you an understanding of what they need to get to where they need to be. Their explanation doesn't excuse underperformance. They still have goals to hit. But when you combine alerting them to their short-comings and understanding why they are falling short, it sends a clear message that even though they are not hitting the target right now, you want to help them get there.

That caring approach preserves their ego and tells them that you want them to be successful, both in working for you and in their life outside of work. It also shows that you understand what matters to them and what they need and that you are willing to support them. Delivering hard feedback in this way, with grace, can make an otherwise uncomfortable and dreaded conversation into an exciting and motivational one simply because it keeps the underperformer's views and needs front and center.

Let them take the lead.

Some employees are truly motivated by showcasing their skills. They may want to take on a project to demonstrate how worthy they are of a promotion, fulfilling their sense of self-worth and their appetite for career growth. Allowing an employee to take the lead on a project might also act as an opportunity for them to demonstrate to you why they are deserving of a higher-than-average merit increase during the next round of performance reviews. Leading a project might feed an intrinsic motivation for survival through higher income from a promotion, or it could tap into a drive tied to their sense of self by appealing to their ego.

In contrast, some may also find pride simply in knowing that they were able to contribute to a project that added value in some way, regardless of how it may have propelled their career. For example, a fundraising project that raised money for children with cancer might be a cause that resonates with a person who has suffered the loss of a relative to this terrible disease. Providing them an opportunity—an opportunity availed to them by working for you—might feed a fire of motivation to contribute to helping others not feel the pain and loss that they experienced.

Letting others take the lead also might make some people feel needed. I once had an assistant who had been with the company for a very long time. She had been in an administrative role prior to an organizational restructuring, and because her role was eliminated, she was retained as an assistant to the HR manager. We will call this assistant Grace.

Grace knew that she was approaching retirement age. She was not interested in pursuing career advancement, and she was not chasing a higher salary. Grace was at a different stage in life, one where she knew that she would soon have to leave the working world and step into retirement. To her, the destination meant stepping away from the one place where she knew she was needed and where people looked to her for guidance. That realization was hard for her to wrestle with. She wasn't ready to leave the workforce because without it, she didn't know her purpose. So, when I asked her to take the lead on something, she got joy out of it not because of the accolades attached, but because she felt needed. Any project she led she drove with passion, and that was because it fulfilled her motivational SPARK.

Keep the good stuff coming.

Wouldn't we all like to step into our dream jobs right now? You know the job I am talking about. The perfect job with the perfect schedule and the healthy, guaranteed salary. The one that comes with perks galore, a generous pension, and maybe even early retirement.

Well, I am not going to burst your bubble and tell you that the job you're thinking of doesn't exist. It very well might. I am all for your going after it! But it will never be perfect all the time. Every job, no matter what it is, comes with aspects we love and ones we don't. A CEO might be passionate about growing a brand and building unprecedented profits. That focus may feel like they are in their dream job. Yet that same CEO might hate business accounting. Still, understanding the budget and being able to dissect their monetary flow through financial tools are necessary aspects to their role.

Every job, no matter the level, comes with things we love and things we don't. A key trick to building motivated, high-performing teams is to maintain an awareness of what I call the work/drive balance. To stay driven, we all have to be able to dedicate aspects of our workdays, or at least our workweek, to parts of our jobs that we love.

I have spent decades in leadership and human resources. What that translates to is that I have spent countless hours of my life listening to disgruntled employees complain about all the things that they hate, how unfair things are, and how they have been wronged. While this time has allowed me to extract the highly coveted raw and honest employee voice, which I am extraordinarily grateful for, it has also been very taxing. Listening to employees complain can suck the life out of you. It can get depressing.

If I were to be completely honest, if the intake of employee complaints was the only aspect of my job, I don't think I would have lasted very long. The job would have been too daunting. What has kept me going all these years is the ability to take that feedback and curate content that can be helpful to managers who are struggling. That aspect of my job is what fulfills my soul—so much so that if I go too long without creating some sort of training to help managers become more effective, I start to lose my SPARK. My motivation plummets, and I no longer want to listen intently. When I find myself in this spot, I have to create a project that adds value. I look for voids in a market and curate content to help fill them. That addition of the work I love—the good stuff—injects an instant dose of motivation back into my job. I feel a renewed sense of passion and loyalty to the brand.

The same concept applies to your team. To maintain a driven and passionate team, you will need to know what they love the most about their jobs and ensure a balance of that in their day-to-days. Make sure you are feeding that motivational fire with constant tasks that tie into that SPARK.

Although you want to keep the good work flowing, be mindful of how many tasks you give at once. Everyone has different thresholds for workload, and employees won't always speak up when they start to feel overwhelmed. If they feel like you expect more from them than they can confidently take on, they will stop trying.

And what a team member loves about their job doesn't always have to be related to their specific job description. It might be interaction with a specific person or team (a waitress with her regulars is a perfect example). It might be having a fixed schedule so that they can plan their time outside of work. Or it might be having a flexible schedule that allows them the ability to adapt to their children's changing needs. Make sure to protect whatever aspect of the job a person appreciates and enjoys the most. Keep giving them access to what they see as the good stuff, and they will continue to meet your dedication with theirs.

The Reciprocal Impact of a Quick Check-In.

It is no secret that employees perform at their best when they feel seen. This is because when our employees feel seen, they feel a sense of belonging which, in turn, makes them feel valued. One of the quickest and most effective ways to help an employee feel seen is to simply check in. Follow up with them to solicit an update on what they previously shared with you is important to them—a project, their family, a big event in their life. A simple question of "How is _______ going?" sends a clear message that you see and are interested in what they care about. So, knowing what we now know about personal motives and motivation at work, it should come as no surprise that something as simple as a quick check-in to follow up on what you have already identified as important is a simple yet powerful way to ignite motivation.

I will never forget Ally. She is a perfect example of how a simple check-in on something that holds individual value to a person, even if it has nothing to do with the job, can catapult performance and drive.

Ally was a single mom, and her oldest was ready to go to college. Ally had spent a full year helping him research majors and colleges and write college applications, and recently, they had toured his top picks. The entire process was overwhelming and very time-consuming. John, Ally's boss, became aware of the huge undertaking that Ally was helping her son with because he noticed the close clustering of time-off requests and asked her if she had any big plans coming up that she needed to prepare for. After John used some intentional calibrated questions, Ally shared the journey that she had been on with her son.

John knew how important her son's future was to Ally. She was using all her time off to help him complete applications and tour colleges. Her eyes lit up with pride when she talked about how great his grades were or discussed the college major he was interested in. It was clear that the time spent with her son was a very important part of her life that she would never have a chance to redo, and she didn't want to miss a moment of it.

Because he could see how much it meant to her, John made sure to approve all time off so that Ally could have this once-in-a-lifetime experience with her boy. But he didn't stop there. After every college tour, John asked what school they were headed out to see next, and when Ally got back, he asked her what they had thought. The conversations weren't long ones, just a minute or so. But John made sure to check in with Ally on the process whenever their paths crossed.

Every time John initiated a check-in with Ally, she felt as though he truly cared about how important being with her son through these experiences was. She knew he didn't have to check in. And, frankly, most bosses would be annoyed at the amount of time Ally needed off in such a small window. Ally appreciated that when she saw John in the hallway, he remembered how important this was to her and took interest in hearing updates. Because of John's genuine interest, she felt a duty to step up for him in the same way he stepped up for her when she needed it.

Ally stayed loyal to John as one of his top-performing employees until he retired. To this day, Ally remembers John. His check-ins had a lasting impact on her. She describes him as the most caring and supportive boss she ever worked for. She would have moved mountains for him. It wasn't because he gave huge bonuses or a substantial raise each year. It wasn't because he got her ready to be the next person to promote. It was simply because of a couple quick check-ins on what mattered to her during a particular time in her life.

That awkward silence before a meeting starts is uncomfortable and causes the team to take longer to open up, if they do at all. Bypass that stage by checking in with them on what you know their motivators to be: How are the kids? Did they go hiking this weekend? How are the Yankees doing this season?

Bring outside motivation in.

Brian was an incredibly talented salesperson. He prospected more than any other salesperson in the company and broke records year after year. Every year, the executive team looked at Brian as a potential manager, someone who could run teams and recreate himself to produce a team of people as productive as he was. But he didn't have much interest in that. The truth was that he was properly placed in his role and had no ambition to move into another role in the company. He enjoyed coming in, doing his job, feeling as though he had a sense of control over his income (he was paid on commission), and then going home to his family.

You see, working in sales is a hard job. In sales, you hear "no" and get hung up on far more often than you hear "yes," let alone "thank you." It is a grind every day, and sometimes it can get deflating. Brian's boss, Matt, had been in the industry a long time and knew how defeating sales could be, so he made a point to bring some life into the office in ways that had nothing to do with sales. He intentionally found ways to weave outside passions into the office so that external motivation, things that made his people happy, was available to them and shared with the rest of the team.

His way of bringing the outside in with Brian was original.

Brian had an obsession with coffee. He considered himself a coffee connoisseur, if there is such a thing. One morning, Matt, holding a fresh cup of coffee, came to Brian's desk, where he kept a small but industrial-grade espresso machine. "Want a cup?" Brian asked Matt.

Matt looked down at his mug of commoner-grade drip coffee and said, "Actually, yes! Our coffee is garbage. Let me taste yours!" The coffee Brian made was a phenomenal cup of coffee, and it gave Matt an idea.

A couple of weeks later, Matt asked Brian if he was up for a project. He told Brian how impressed he had been with his coffee and how he had been thinking about upgrading the pot in the office, but he didn't know what was good and what wasn't. He asked Brian if he would be up for creating a self-serve coffee bar in the communal lunch area. Brian was beyond ecstatic. He asked Matt for the budget for this project, immediately accepted, and started researching.

Brian, who never brought work home, started spending hours researching the options out there. After a couple of weeks, he had put together a beautiful assortment of high-grade drip coffee, espresso options, and a cold brew. He even went as far as to send out coffee bar menus to the office the week before a new shipment of beans came in.

The coffee bar was all the rage, complete with a grand opening. Brian was over the moon to share his passion with a group of people who truly appreciated his expertise in something that had nothing to do with sales. That little element of fun and joy counteracted the otherwise tumultuous and draining atmosphere the sales industry could create in the office. Recognizing Brian's passion and bringing it in to the workplace was not only a win for Brian, it was a win for the whole team, and it got Matt's team producing at a higher rate than they had been before the coffee bar success. Mission accomplished.

Reap the rewards.

Once you have connected to your employee's SPARK, they will be inspired to work for you and they will want to make you proud. They will feel seen, heard, and supported by you and your company. This will deter them from even considering leaving for another company because they will be gratified with where they are, knowing that you understand them and have their back. That trust will also fire up motivation while they're on the job, creating a team full of drive, pride, and productivity—which, of course, is every manager's dream.

Instead of spending all of your time talking about mission statements and purpose, find what matters to your people by following the first four steps of SPARK, and then get ready for the success that you and your team will see with this last step: Know How to Connect.

Dedicate a little time each day to the SPARK Method, and the dividends will be plentiful.

Key Takeaways:

- Connecting your work to your employees' motives is not a full-time job. It simply takes small tweaks to the things that you probably already do.
- Use recognition strategically.
- Reward them the way *they* want to be rewarded.
- Implement their ideas.
- Approach their mistakes as learnings, not failures.
- Deliver feedback with grace.
- Let them take the lead with ideas or projects that they are passionate about.

- Be mindful of balancing the workload scale with just the mundane, and make sure their days include the things they love to do.
- Check in to remind them that you see them and you care.
- For those who are passionate about something unrelated to your industry, find ways to incorporate their passion outside of work into the work environment.

Step 5 on a Page

Traditionally, we have thought that employees' paychecks are their motivation. That is outdated thinking because there are too many options for how to make money.

When we rely only on money as a means of motivation, employee effort becomes transactional and short term.

The key to igniting long-term, lasting motivation is knowing how to connect what matters to employees to you or to the work they do.

There are two main ways to do this:
- Help them protect what they already care about.
- Give them the tools to attain what they want.

To do this, consider the options that you already have—or could have—to fulfill the things that matter the most to them:
- Flexible scheduling
- Discounts
- Benefits packages
- Paid time off
- Training

Also, consider how to adjust the way you plan, speak to the team, or delegate so as to fulfill their drivers:
- Let them take the lead on a project.
- Use recognition strategically.
- Seek and implement their ideas.
- Bring outside motivation in.
- Check in on what they care about often to show them that you see them.

Once you have identified the type of work that fuels their motivation, make sure they can do it regularly so as to continuously fuel their drive.

You've Got This!

AS YOU BEGIN to implement the SPARK Method, there is a very important point to remember: it is new to you.

And like with anything new, you will stumble along the way at first. There might be points where you overlooked an opportunity to slow down. You might find yourself reflecting on a conversation with a team member and suddenly thinking of a question that would have been a really good one to ask. And there may be times that you overlook an opportunity to connect your work to a team member's SPARK.

But that's okay.

There is no such thing as failure, only lessons. So stop and ask yourself, "What did I learn? What might I be able to try differently?"

Wait until you have left for the day to figure out the answer so that you can think clearly without distractions. Maybe think about it on your drive home or when you're winding down from the week. Replay in your head how you implemented the SPARK Method.

+ Which steps did you implement?
+ What signs did your employees send out? Did you miss any? Or could you have misinterpreted any?
+ What was the quality of your calibrated questions? Could you have rephrased or asked better questions?
+ Were there any clues that you didn't identify in the moment, but now, thinking about it, employees showed?

+ Do you think you identified their SPARK?
+ What questions did you ask to find out if this was *the* thing that mattered to them the most (or at least enough to SPARK action)?
+ Did you maybe misidentify the root driver?
+ Could there be a deeper connection to one of the other motivating drivers? For example, is Connection their driver, or does it seem like they seek connection because they have a low self-esteem, and their *real* driver is their Sense of Self, self-worth?

Once you have mulled over your implementation of the SPARK Method and identified some things you may have been able to do differently, do what every successful manager does: start again. Be tenacious in your pursuit to build a kick-ass team. If you want to succeed, you have to keep going.

Now, I realize that the process can be exhausting. It can feel defeating when you have tried so hard but didn't get the results that you hoped for. So, how do you cope with that disappointment? How do you find the strength to keep going?

The answer: Motivation. Yours.

And, lucky for you, you now have an intricate understanding of what drives motivation. We are all motivated by how a behavior might directly support or protect the things that significantly matter to us. You are no different. So, when you find yourself lacking drive and motivation to keep going, consider how finding and connecting to their SPARK helps you attain what matters to *you!*

Have you ever thought about which of the three motivational drivers is at the root of your own motivation? What is that thing for you? Connection? Survival? Or your sense of self?

If you aren't completely sure, or if you are curious and want to verify, consider how you might answer the following questions:

+ If you had to work a double shift at the last minute, how would that make you feel? Would you be angry because you would have to miss another dinner with your family? Or would you be excited because it meant more money in your paycheck?
+ When you put a lot of effort into a project, what gesture of appreciation would motivate you the most? A shout-out by your boss on a team call? A gift card? Some comp time?
+ If you did get some extra comp time, what would you do with it? Would you look for a new place to live? Would you spend time with friends? Would you plan your next vacation? Would you read articles about business development or a book about how to motivate your team?

To light the motivational fire within you, it's essential for you to connect the implementation of the SPARK Method to what matters the most to you. Ask yourself:

+ What would a motivated, high-performing team do for you?
+ How might it change your life?
+ Would you have less stress?

+ Would you go home in a better mood and be able to enjoy time with your family?
+ Would you be able to get some sort of social life back?
+ Would it enable you to keep your job so that you could keep your salary and keep a roof over your head?
+ Would you get the recognition and promotion that you have been after?

Whatever successfully implementing the SPARK Method will help you to fulfill, write that thing down and make it visible. Put it on a sticky note on your bathroom mirror. Make it the home screen on your phone. Set a reminder on your calendar so that the reason flashes across your desktop once a week. Having a regular reminder will help you connect your regular application of the SPARK Method to your SPARK.

And because you are aware of the positive payout waiting for you on the other side of a motivated and high-performing team, you will find the will to keep going.

No matter how many times it takes, it will be worth it.

Acknowledgements

Ever since my first leadership role I have always said: Every human should, at some point in their lives, be required to work in the service industry - the world would be a better place. And, I mean it. The entire human race would benefit from experiencing firsthand just how hard it is to deal with and manage people. It is a ruthless, and sometimes thankless job. But, the world is better off because of those leaders who continue to dedicate their careers to learning, growing, and improving their ability to have a positive influence on others. Thank you to every leader who commits to invest in their growth. Leadership is a lifestyle, and you are the force that shapes it. Keep going.

And, of course, my tribe. Writing a book is the hardest thing I have ever done. My boys, Collin and AJ, are my never-ending inspiration. They are the reason I choose to keep going, even when times get hard. You are my SPARK, and I am grateful for you every day.

To my husband, who held down the fort during my many, many hours of writing at the local coffee shop, thank you for always believing in me and giving me the space to create and accomplish my goals. I love you.

And to my girls. The ones who always have my back, never judge, and support unconditionally, you are priceless and I am grateful that life brought us together.

Finally, The Book Launchers team, and Bev, who kept it real, told me what I needed to hear, and kept me on point – you are phenomenal, and I wouldn't have made it to the finish line without you.

LET'S SPARK MOTIVATION
TOGETHER!

Burnt out? Frustrated? Download my free
5 Day Mindset Reset for managers at
www.jcbernstein.net/online-resources

For special discounts on bulk book purchases, contact
crescentheightspublishing.com

To book JC for speaking events or team masterclasses,
visit **jcbernstein.net/get-mentored**

For more free tips, subscribe to JC's YouTube Channel
@themanagementmentor

THANK YOU FOR READING!

If you enjoyed **IGNITE YOUR TEAM**,
please leave a review on Goodreads or on the retailer
site where you purchased this book
and help me reach more readers like you!

* 9 7 9 8 9 8 7 5 2 1 2 0 5 *